D0014494

KILL OR CAPTURE

ALSO BY MATTHEW ALEXANDER

How to Break a Terrorist: The U.S. Interrogators Who Used Brains, Not Brutality, to Take Down the Deadliest Man in Iraq

KILL OR CAPTURE

How a Special Operations Task Force Took
Down a Notorious al Qaeda Terrorist

Matthew Alexander

St. Martin's Press New York

www.stmartins.com

Library of Congress Cataloging-in-Publication Data

Alexander, Matthew, 1970–
    Kill or capture : how a special operations task force took down a notorious al Qaeda terrorist / Matthew Alexander.—1st ed.
        p. cm.
    ISBN 978-0-312-65687-4
    1. Iraq War, 2003—Commando operations.   2. Iraq War, 2003—Personal narratives, American.   3. Special operations (Military science)—Iraq.   4. Military interrogation—Iraq.   5. Qaida (Organization)   6. Insurgency—Iraq.   7. United States. Army. Special Forces—History—Iraq War, 2003–   8. Alexander, Matthew, 1970–   I. Title.
    DS79.766.A54A3 2011
    956.7044'38—dc22

                                                            2010039357

First Edition: February 2011

10 9 8 7 6 5 4 3 2 1

To the heroes of this war—
the soldiers we lost in the hunt

CONTENTS

Contents

AUTHOR'S NOTE

KILL OR CAPTURE

Chasing Terrorists

I get asked all the time, "What's it like chasing terrorists?" Well, there's never a dull moment. Every time you think you've seen it all, there's a new twist. You sit down in front of a guy who just cut somebody's head off with a machete, make friends with him and, surprise, you learn he's a human being. Killer by day, family man by night. After he cleans the blood off his blade, he goes home at night, eats dinner with the family, tells a joke at the supper table, and tucks his kids into bed. I think that's what Americans don't understand. To the Sunnis we were fighting in Iraq who decided to join al Qaeda, what they were doing was honorable. They were fighting. I'll never condone their tactics, but I understood *why* they were fighting, and because I understood why they were fighting, I could get them to talk. How? By using that information against them. When Sun Tzu said, "Know thy self, know thy enemy, a thousand battles, a thousand victories," he wasn't bullshitting. Interrogations are all about knowing yourself and your enemy. Or, I would argue, *transforming* yourself and your enemy.

The best interrogators are one-third salesman, one-third dramatic actor, and one-third psychologist. They are the most able to adapt to the detainee's world—and then to transform it. I can become a father, a brother, a husband, or a friend . . . whatever it takes to convince a detainee to talk. This is about getting information, not retribution or punishment. An effective interrogation is not a harsh interrogation. Words like "soft" and "hard" mean nothing to me—either an interrogation yields accurate and timely intelligence or it doesn't.

The techniques we use must be in accordance with our values and principles. We are Americans and we must fight like Americans. When we face adversity we do what Americans have always done: We improvise, adapt, and overcome. What we don't do is break the law. We cannot become our enemy in trying to defeat him.

There are several legendary American interrogators. Men you've never heard of who achieved greatness in this often misunderstood profession. Men like Major Sherwood Moran, who spent forty years in Japan as a missionary before signing up for the marines in his fifties during World War II. Moran convinced numerous Japanese prisoners of war to talk. How was he able to do his job against an enemy so dedicated to their emperor that they were willing to be suicide bombers? In Moran's own words, an interrogator needs to be a real "wooer." Another World War II interrogator, Technical Sergeant Grant Hirabayashi (a Japanese American Nisei soldier), also used relationship-building approaches to great success while assigned to Merrill's Marauders, fighting across Burma.

On the other front, a secretive interrogation unit at Virginia's Fort Hunt, better known as PO Box 1142, successfully interrogated high-level German prisoners. Their arsenal? Cigarettes and chess. They never laid a hand on a detainee, but they got them to talk by getting to know them.

In Vietnam, Orrin DeForest, a former military criminal investigator, made a name for himself by incorporating his law enforcement skills into his work as a CIA interrogator. He taught South Vietnamese soldiers how to use noncoercive relationship-building approaches and combined that with a meticulous system of manual data collection. Halfway through the war, for the first time, the United States was able to form a clear picture of the Vietcong's operational architecture in South Vietnam. Another Vietnam legend, Colonel Stuart Herrington, also successfully interrogated numerous prisoners using these techniques.

A history of great interrogators would be incomplete without mentioning Hanns Scharff, a German Luftwaffe interrogator in World War II. Many an Allied pilot un-wittingly divulged information to Scharff because of his ability to put prisoners at ease with his good manners. Again, it was relationship-building approaches and a de-tailed informational database that led to Scharff's suc-cess. Scharff became an American citizen after the war and a respected mosaic artist. His work is still on display at California's Disneyland.

After 9/11, the U.S. government forgot its rich history of conducting humane (and successful) interrogations based on relationship building. It was too easy to indulge in hate for our enemies and give in to the desire for retri-bution following the tragedy of that day. We invaded Af-ghanistan, rightly I believe, but the interrogators there found the methods in the Army Field Manual ineffective against detainees. It's not surprising why. They didn't un-derstand the culture of the men they faced. These weren't the Cold War soldiers they were trained to interrogate. Frustrated by the lack of intelligence information coming from interrogators, the Bush administration turned to so-called experts, who had never conducted an interroga-tion. They decided to "take the gloves off," abandoning decades of military interrogation knowledge and tradi-tion. The torture and abuse of prisoners was approved at the highest levels of government and encouraged by se-nior military leaders, in complete contradiction to the military's own doctrine, training, and tradition.

Then came the invasion of Iraq. The army was stretched and the pool of interrogators ran dry. So they called the air force and the air force called me. For the second time in my career, I put away my surfboard, buzzed my sunbleached hair, and volunteered to go to the war in Iraq.

In war, you get swallowed up, especially when every day you are going outside the wire chasing terrorists. The hunt becomes all consuming. You eat, drink, and sleep it. When we had an hour here or there to run to the chow hall, our conversations drifted to interrogations and detainees. We discussed sleights of hand in convincing detainees to talk. We debated how to improve the methods, adding new twists, but we also discussed the personal lives of the men we captured. Who were they? Why were they fighting? Why were we here? Were we making a difference? We knew that for every terrorist leader we captured or killed, there were ten ready to take his place. In ten or twenty years, would anyone care about what we were doing?

It's been said that in war, you don't fight for your country or for a cause. You fight for the guy next to you. Well, that's true, and any one of us would have gone to great lengths to defend the other, but I felt as if I was also fighting for someone else. I felt like a protector. A protector of the Iraqi mother who walks her daughter to the market, only to end up another statistic on a pie chart. A protector of the father, a taxi driver who's in the wrong place at the wrong time when a roadside bomb goes off and loses both legs. A protector of the female journalist punctured twenty times by a power drill before being decapitated. Those are the people I feel I'm fighting for. Do I fight for my country? Damn right I do. Do I fight for the soldier next to me? Hell, yes. Yet how do I feel in the middle of the chase for a terrorist? I feel like there are a thousand Iraqis out there right now who have no idea that tomorrow they will be blown to bits if we don't find our target tonight. For those innocent civilians, I'm also going to fight.

We can talk about national security, weapons of mass destruction, safe havens for terrorists, and all the other political mumbo jumbo, but in the heat of the moment, in the midst of the chase, what drives me most is the image of a little girl lying in the street charred beyond recognition. I want to catch the bastard who did it and stop him from ever doing it again.

In the summer of 2006, that bastard had a name. It was Zafar—and I was coming for him.

1

The Mole

May 15, 2006
Kirkuk, Iraq

A solitary streetlight casts the black shadows of the soldiers against a stone wall. The soldiers kneel, their rifles in the ready position, and wave green infrared beams, scanning rooftops, windows, and balconies, until the silence is broken by a whisper yelled over the wall.

"Clear!"

A small explosion is followed by the sound of metal falling onto stone. Two of the soldiers kneeling against the wall stand and rush through the metal gate, through the courtyard, and into the house, followed closely by an interrogator, hoping to grab evidence before it can be flushed. Inside the doorway, Zafar's men greet the team with a death chime.

"Allah Akhbar!"

Two human bombs detonate, turning the inside of the

house into a maelstrom of fire and shrapnel. The soldiers and suicide bombers die instantly, engulfed in scraps of hot metal and flames, and the interrogator is blown off the porch and lands on his back in the courtyard. Everything goes black as blood pours down his face and hands grab his arms and legs and lift him into the air. He opens his eyes and sees the clear night sky filled with thousands of stars.

Meanwhile, a man escapes out the back door of the house, but before he can take ten steps he is tackled and tied by a soldier. The soldier sits the man in the sand and kneels to face him.

"Hello, Mahmoud. Going somewhere?"

May 22, 2006
Central Iraq

I listen to the wail of the horn as the bugle player at the front of the formation, decked out in full army dress, puffs out the long and solemn notes. We are a formation of camouflage uniforms and civilian clothes, standing at attention in crisp rank and file to honor our fallen comrades. They are not the first that our task force has lost in this hunt.

In the distance, mortars, like soft drums, land and shake the compound, growing closer every second, but not a soul moves in the formation. We will not be deterred from honoring our fallen comrades.

Mahmoud is a delicate man with tiny features, short brown hair, and a trimmed beard. It's hard to imagine this diminutive Syrian as the number two man behind al Qaeda's northern campaign of violence, but it takes brains, not muscles, to fight an insurgency.

We captured Mahmoud in a raid in Kirkuk a week ago. He was caught in a house/factory used for the production of suicide vests and we knew full well who he was when we captured him—he had been on the Most Wanted list for months. Mahmoud runs the suicide bombing operations for al Qaeda in northern Iraq and the analysts say he reports directly to Zafar, a shadow of a man who exists only in rumors and recently took the lives of two of our brothers-in-arms. There are no pictures of Zafar and no one has admitted to meeting him, but several detainees have confirmed that he is the leader of al Qaeda in the north. He is Iraq's Keyser Söze, and we hope that Mahmoud will lead us to him. This is how we found Abu Musab al-Zarqawi, by slowly and methodically climbing the ladder of al Qaeda leadership.

Mahmoud sits in a white plastic chair in a plywood-walled interrogation room. In front of him sit two interrogators who specialize in foreign fighters. They are both in their midthirties, with long unkempt beards grown over the past three months. As the task force's senior interrogator, I supervise from the Hollywood Room next door, an observation room with rows of monitors. The interrogation takes place in English.

"Tell me about Zafar," the black-bearded interrogator asks.

"I don't know anyone named Zafar," Mahmoud answers.

"Don't lie to us!" the brown-bearded interrogator shouts. "You know who the fuck we're talking about!"

Mahmoud stares at the interrogator with a blank look on his face.

"*Wallah mawf,*" he says flatly.

I don't know.

Brownbeard throws his notebook on the floor, stands, and walks up to the seated Mahmoud. The top of the Syrian's head barely comes to the interrogator's waist.

"Listen to me, you little shit," he says, "you're going to hang for what you've done, and the only way to avoid the noose is to work with us. You understand?"

In the monitor room I shake my head. These interrogators don't belong to me. I monitor their interrogations out of courtesy, but they've never followed the advice I've offered. They are old school.

Mahmoud shrugs his shoulders. Brownbeard turns and slams his fist against the wall.

"Motherf—"

"Listen," Blackbeard interrupts, "we're trying to help you here. We can work together. You help us and we'll help you."

It's a classic Good Cop/Bad Cop approach, but the Bad Cop should be outside the room so that the detainee feels comfortable confiding in the nice guy. Still, I admire Blackbeard's attempt to build rapport.

"I don't want your help," Mahmoud replies. "Unless . . ."

"Unless what?!" Brownbeard yells.

"Unless you want to release me to find this man named Zafar."

"I thought you said you didn't know a Zafar!"

"Perhaps my memory will improve once I am out of this prison."

"You little shit! We should—"

"Wait," Blackbeard interrupts again. "Do you mean that if we let you go then you can find Zafar for us?"

"It's possible," Mahmoud says.

"How would you go about doing that?"

Mahmoud casually waves his hand as he speaks.

"I know people. I can ask around. Then I can call you when I find him."

"But al Qaeda knows you've been captured!" Brownbeard says. "Why the hell would they trust you?"

"Do you think that I would be the first fighter that you have accidentally released?" Mahmoud replies.

Mahmoud is correct. Last month I flew to a base in western Iraq to help interrogate five men captured in a house that U.S. forces thought was used to train suicide bombers, but the house was empty of evidence. None of the five men revealed any information and we had no reason to believe they were involved with the insurgency, other than an anonymous tip that was provided to us. The decision was made to release the five men because the tip, it was suspected, was a vindictive false report—a common occurrence. We pushed the men out the front gate of the base and I gave one of them twenty dollars out of my own pocket for a taxi. Two weeks later we recaptured the same man—this time in a house with bombs. The moral of the story: Counterinsurgency is complex.

"How long would it take you to find Zafar?" Blackbeard asks.

"A week," Mahmoud answers.

"What if we release you and you run?" Brownbeard asks.

"You know where my family lives," Mahmoud answers. "You caught me in my house."

The two interrogators look at each other. Blackbeard nods toward the door.

"We'll be back in a moment," he says to Mahmoud and the two men convene outside and close the door.

I leave the Hollywood Room and join them in the hallway.

"Do you think the Colonel will go for it?" Blackbeard asks.

"I don't know," Brownbeard replies. "I don't trust this guy and I don't know how I'm going to convince the Colonel to trust him."

Blackbeard turns to me.

"What do you think?"

I consider it. We've never done this before that I know of, but I'm all for trying new things. Even if Mahmoud doesn't lead us to Zafar, he might kick up some dust in his wake that we can follow.

"In the criminal world we run dirty sources all the time," I say. "It's part of the business."

Blackbeard nods and Brownbeard defers to me.

"Go for it," I say. "See what the Colonel thinks."

Later that day the two interrogators meet with the Colonel. The mission gets approved, with caveats. Mahmoud is to be monitored closely and the entire operation is to be strictly controlled. If he runs, the first order of business will be to shoot him. The entire time he is free, Big Brother will be watching.

2

Go North

June 8, 2006
Central Iraq

Zarqawi is one dead son of a bitch. The mastermind
behind Iraq's civil war is spread out at my feet, bloated
and swaddled, a white sheet wrapped around his groin.
The blood that he was so fond of spilling is smeared
across his cheek, but even as the news spreads across the
globe, the suicide bombings in Iraq continue. There is no
time to rejoice as al Qaeda in Iraq has already announced
a new leader—Abu Ayyub al-Masri, the Egyptian—and
their plan to renew the fight in the north is well under-
way. They have given up on Baghdad, which is now firmly
in Shi'a hands. Muqtada al-Sadr and his Mahdi Army,
wearing their landmark bright green headbands, flowed
out of Sadr City and across Baghdad's neighborhoods,
ensuring that the capital stayed in the Shi'a win column.

Anbar Province may soon follow. Word on the street

is that we are negotiating with the Sunni tribes. The marines have already struck deals with some influential sheikhs in Ramadi. Yusifiya, the farmland southwest of Baghdad and al Qaeda's former safe haven, has been ravaged. Unknown to the leaders of the insurgency, my team of 'gators had a long talk with a twelve-year-old boy with a habit for braggadocio who laid out their suicide bombing network across the province—their base for Baghdad operations.

For more than three years our elite task force chased Zarqawi, losing brave men in the pursuit. At the time of his death he was the most wanted terrorist on the planet, a higher priority than Osama bin Laden. For months the chase consumed every second of my life, yet I feel but half triumphant.

We gained valuable intelligence from raids conducted on the night of Zarqawi's death and the intelligence points to an ominous cloud on the horizon. The Jordanian preacher of hate left a final message to his subordinates in a letter found on a laptop in a Baghdad apartment. Al Qaeda has lost Baghdad and the Sunni sheikhs of Anbar Province are meeting with the Americans. Deals are in the making. Three prominent Sunni insurgent groups (Ansar al-Sunnah, the 1920 Revolution Brigades, and the Islamic Army in Iraq) have already split from al Qaeda to form their own coalition. In essence, the western provinces of Iraq are lost.

In the past, al Qaeda proved to be a Hydra—the snake grew new heads as quickly as we chopped them off—but with the Sunnis abandoning al Qaeda's foreign leadership, there is a brief opportunity for a devastating decapitation before they can regroup. Al Qaeda's brutality, especially toward its own fighters, is returning to haunt it. Some of our best sources are former al Qaeda religious leaders who have rejected their violent methods. Al Qaeda is an injured predator, hobbled and backed into a corner, but vicious. Suicide bombings and beheadings are still daily occurrences.

Zarqawi's final order before his death is clear: Go north, regroup, and live to fight another day. Kirkuk, Mesopotamia's ancient Assyrian capital, will be al Qaeda's last stand. The last of the insurgency's butchers plan to cling to this final stronghold. Rooting them out will be no less than diving into a hornets' nest.

I return to my sand-covered desk in the 'Gator Pit, our end-of-the-world office space, and pick up a report. We still have prisoners to interrogate and I have interrogators to advise and reports to review. As the senior interrogator for the task force, I've run a team of a dozen interrogators for the past two months. We put together a string of successes and convinced a Zarqawi associate to sell him out. Along the way, we abandoned the old-school methods of interrogation (those developed at Guantanamo Bay and early on in Afghanistan) based on fear and control, and instead set a new path using techniques based on relationship building, cultural understanding, negotiation, and intellect. It's been a stunning upset by my group of interrogators, and the evidence of the effectiveness of our new methods lay last night at my feet.

"Matthew!"

I turn around and see Roger, the interrogation unit commander, addressing me from the doorway to his office. I shiver for a second at the thought that perhaps he has somehow discovered the end around I pulled on everyone by striking a secret deal with the detainee who gave us the path to Zarqawi—actions that I felt were necessary to circumvent the micromanagement of my interrogations team.

"Sir?" I answer.

"I need to talk to you in my office," Roger says.

I drop the report in my hand and walk into Roger's office. He closes the door behind me.

"Your request has been granted," Roger says.

"To go north?" I ask.

"Yes," he replies. "You're leaving tomorrow at seventeen hundred to join a raid team. Go home and pack your bags. Good luck, and try not to get blown up."

He means that literally. I say thanks and make my way back to my desk. I clean up some reports, stroll the hallway between the plywood interrogation rooms one last time, checking to make sure they are clean for the incoming shift, and then make for my trailer. My day started at nine in the morning and it is now past midnight. It's been nonstop like this since I arrived in Iraq over three months ago.

As I walk on the orange sand between the concrete Jersey barriers, I reflect upon the past three months. Everything I learned at the interrogation schoolhouse at Fort Huachuca has been turned on its head. Along with my team, I've sharpened my ability to evaluate detainees and polished the doppelganger that I transform into every time I step onto the stage. Now, I'm ready to take these skills north and apply them in a more challenging, and dangerous, environment. I'm going to join a raid team and conduct interrogations at the point-of-capture, attempting to find the next target as quickly as possible before the enemy can react. Interrogating in a prison is challenging and there is significant pressure to elicit information quickly, but the environment is mostly static. The stakes are about to be raised. In my new role, I won't have hours or days to get information—I'll have minutes.

Last month we lost two soldiers to suicide bombers when they rushed into a house during a raid. An interrogator assigned to the team took shrapnel to the face. Replacing that interrogator was my good friend Mike, a former street cop and Cajun, who, like me, is an air force criminal investigator turned interrogator charged with helping this elite task force. Tomorrow I'll head north to join Mike and, together with two Iraqi interpreters, we will be the Mobile Interrogations Team. I'm about to fly right into the heart of the fight. The last butchers of Iraq have regrouped and at their center is a man that, ironically, I was face-to-face with just weeks ago. He was one of our prisoners, before we let him go.

3

Twins

June 9, 2009
Kirkuk, Iraq

The prop-job lands with a quick bounce on the runway in Kirkuk. We pull off the runway and stop at the edge of the tarmac. It's darker than three feet up a bull's ass. Next to the parking ramp there's an SUV waiting with the lights off. I sling my rifle over my shoulder, grab my duffel bag, and exit the side door. The loadmaster bids me farewell with a short salute.

Mike exits the SUV's driver seat and greets me with a firm handshake. He is muscular, midthirties, and his black hair is just beginning to pepper with gray. He was a street cop, a SWAT sniper, and an attorney before he turned to the air force to run criminal investigations, ultimately landing in Iraq as an interrogator, helping out the army. The task force interrogators are a hodgepodge of active duty, former military, and ex–law enforcement types.

"Good to see you," he says. "You're just in time."

"Just in time for what?" I ask.

"Just in time to go out on a mission. We leave in an hour. We have enough time to get back to our office, throw your bag down, and get your gear on. The rest I'll explain on the way to the target."

An hour later, the rear ramp door of the Stryker personnel carrier closes next to me and the armored vehicle accelerates. Mike sits across from me and gives me a smile.

"Welcome to Kirkuk," he says, "where every day brings a new raid."

I grin as the vehicle turns a corner. A minute later, as we pass through a heavily guarded gate, a crewmember up front turns and yells.

"Lock and load!"

Mike and the two medics sitting next to us rack the slides on their M-4s and the snapping metal echoes through the cabin over the high-pitched whine of the vehicle's engine. I rack the slide on my rifle. We're outside the wire.

It's hot in the back of the Stryker, even with the fan turned on. Six of us are cramped into a sardine-can worth of space. There are two interrogators, two medics, and two Iraqi interpreters: Biggie and Tiny, Shi'a from the south of Iraq who emigrated years ago to the U.S. They're more than interpreters; they're also walking and talking cultural encyclopedias, but they come with a price tag.

Word is that they make a hundred and fifty thousand dollars a year. Probably five times the salary of the Specialist sitting next to me.

As the Stryker hits a bump and turns, our rifles rattle and we bounce off one another.

"When we get to the target, just follow me," Mike says. "Once the team clears the house, then they'll call us in."

It sounds easy enough.

Mike hands me a small slip of paper. I examine it. It's a two-inch by two-inch intelligence card. In the middle is the name of the man we're looking for: Omar. Above his name is the next ring on the ladder: Abu Azir. I fold the piece of paper and place it in my pocket.

"One more thing," he shouts. "When they call for air-guards, open the hatch above your head, stand up through it, and scan for targets."

The Stryker is new to the U.S. Army. It has a crew of three: a driver, a tank commander (called the TC), and a gunner who operates a swivel-mounted .50 caliber machine gun on top. The TC often stands up through a porthole in the middle of the vehicle and directs the driver, guiding him around turns that he can't see, and providing guidance to speed up or slow down in relation to our distance to the Stryker in front of us. The Strykers have proven resistant to most roadside bombs and there's been only one rumored casualty to date. That was a direct hit from underneath by an EFP—Explosively Formed

Projectile—the mother ship of roadside bombs that the Iranians have taught the insurgents to build. Despite the Stryker's impressive record, roadside bombs are always in the back of our minds.

The Stryker slows to a crawl and the TC turns and yells, "Airguards!"

Mike shouts to me, "That's our call! Open your hatch!"

I stand up on the seat and push the thick heavy hatch open. It lands with a thud on the roof of the vehicle. I flip down my night-vision monocle and as I poke my head out of the hatch, I am greeted by a rush of warm air, albeit twenty degrees cooler than the air below. I bring my rifle up through the hole, raise it to the ready position, and flick on the green infrared laser.

We're strolling down a residential street of middle-class homes and I use my laser to illuminate windows and roofs. The street is empty and quiet, except for a few barking dogs. The Stryker formation comes to a halt and I hear garbled radio chatter on the loudspeaker in the crew compartment below. For a minute I continue to scan the rooftops and then the TC calls, " 'Gators!"

I follow Mike's lead and drop down into the crew compartment as the rear hatch lowers. He exits first and I am followed by Biggie and Tiny. We trot down the paved street next to a stone wall and find the raid team kneeling beside a metal gate. Green lasers wave in all directions across the clear night sky. Just as we kneel down next to the wall, a whisper yell is shouted:

"Clear!"

There's an explosion, followed by the sound of metal falling onto stone. The soldiers along the wall stand and rush through the gate. The raid takes less than a minute and then the Alabama Lieutenant in charge of the mission appears at the gate. He's in his late twenties, but he has the slow and deliberate demeanor of an aged Southern gentlemen.

" 'Gators," he says, "we're ready for you. Two adult males in the back room. Twin brothers."

Mike and I follow him into the house, which consists of three rooms made of cinder-block walls and dirt floors. In the back room there are two older men, identical twins, standing against a wall with their hands tied behind their backs.

"We've got these two guys here, and in the room next door are the women and children," the Lieutenant says.

The two men stand side by side, both dressed in filthy white dishdashas and barefoot. They are indeed identical. Both have big guts, large noses, and thick, gray mustaches. I can't tell them apart until I approach and notice that one has a scar under his eye. He looks up at me, but his brother continues to stare at the floor.

"I'll take this one into the front room," I say and grab the one with the scar and lead him away by his arm.

As Biggie follows me, Mike leans over and whispers in my ear, "We only have ten minutes."

I put the scarred brother against a wall in the front room, hold my rifle at my side in one hand, and with the other I lean against the wall next to his head. Our faces are inches apart. Biggie closes in and together we form a box. I wipe at the sweat rolling down my forehead with the back of my hand and push my helmet back on my head. The scarred brother looks down at the ground.

"I want to make this very clear from the start," I say.

I'm whispering and Biggie whispers as he translates my words.

"Do you understand?"

The scarred brother nods and shuffles on his feet. He stinks of body odor and the tiny details of the scar on his face are clear. It's thick and without stitch marks.

"I'm not going to hurt you. I'm just going to ask you some questions and I want you to give me honest answers," I say. "It's too hot for me to stick around here asking things two or three times."

He nods.

"I don't want you to worry about your family. We're not going to hurt them."

The scarred brother glances up at my face and then down again.

"What is your name?" I ask.

"Omar," he says.

"Good," I say. "Who lives in this house?"

"I do," Omar replies.

"Who else?"

"My family."

"What is your wife's name?"

"Nawal."

"How many kids do you have?"

"Three. Two boys and a girl."

"Does anyone else live here?"

"No."

"Who's the man in the other room?"

"My brother."

"What's his name?"

"Fadil."

"Does he stay here?"

"No."

"Is his family here?"

"No. He came alone."

"When did he get here?"

"About one hour ago. He came to eat dinner."

"Did anyone stay here last night?"

"No."

"Has anyone stayed here in the last week?"

"No."

"Do you have any other brothers?"

"No."

I ask additional questions about his family. I write down the names of his father, mother, uncles, and the names of two other distant relatives who live in Kirkuk. None of the names match the one on the intelligence sheet in my top pocket, but this man's name is Omar, just as the intelligence indicated.

"What is your religion?"

"Sunni."

"What is your job?"

"I drive a taxi."

"How long have you driven a taxi?"

"Three months."

Omar shuffles on his feet and rolls his shoulders as best he can with his hands tied behind his back. A strange guttural sound comes from behind me and I step away from Omar, quickly turn, and raise my rifle. An old gray goat is tied up in a corner of the room that I didn't notice on the way in. I look at Biggie and he raises his bushy eyebrows. A soldier who's kneeling in the front doorway, scanning the street, has a laugh. I lower my rifle and return to Omar.

"What did you do before you drove a taxi?"

"I was a teacher."

"What did you teach?"

"Math."

"What grade did you teach?"

"I don't understand," Omar says.

Biggie translates again and Omar answers.

"Years five through ten," Biggie informs me.

"What is your brother's job?"

"He's also a teacher."

"What does he teach?"

"History."

"Does he still teach?"

"No, he doesn't work now."

"Why can't he drive a taxi like you?"

"He doesn't have a car."

"Where is your car?" I ask.

"It's getting fixed at the garage."

"What's wrong with it?"

"The transmission has a problem."

Everyone is worried about car bombs so this peaks my interest. My questions involve a lot of detail, but it will eliminate his brother being able to match his responses with lucky guesses.

"Wait here," I say and leave Omar with Biggie.

I enter the room just as Mike is finishing up; with a nod he follows me to a corner where we put our heads together.

"Any hits on the names?"

"No."

We compare our lists of relatives and they match. Neither has omitted a name, which would be a sign that something is amiss. All of our notes are identical.

"What do you think?" Mike asks. "Wrong house?"

"I don't know," I say. "The intel sheet said that we would find an Omar and my guy's name is Omar."

"Does he know this other target on the sheet, Abu Azir?"

"I haven't asked him the name directly. I don't want to give away who we're looking for."

The Alabama Lieutenant approaches from outside.

"Got anything?" he asks.

Mike and I trade looks.

"I have an Omar and that's the target," I say. "But we haven't gotten anything about our next target, yet."

"How long do you need? It's fuckin' hot," the Lieutenant says as he wipes at his square forehead.

"Give us five more minutes," Mike says.

"Alright, five minutes, but let me know if you get anything before that."

"Will do," I say and the Lieutenant walks outside.

Mike looks at me.

"Do you have any ideas?" I ask.

"Prisoner's dilemma," he replies.

Mike is reaching into his bag of old street-cop tricks. When you catch two suspects in a criminal act and separate them, they are at a disadvantage because they don't know what the other is saying. One suspect has to trust the other not to talk or take a deal. It only takes the slightest bit of cooperation from one to make the other lose faith, and then the entire house of cards comes crashing down.

"How do you want to do it?" I ask.

"Let's both say that the other brother claimed to have a relative named Abu Azir and see if either one breaks," Mike says.

"It's a gamble," I reply. "And we'll be showing our cards by giving them the name of our target."

"Yeah, but what the hell," Mike says. "We have nothing else."

Mike is correct. It's one of the most important lessons we're learning about interrogations in Iraq: When you have nothing to go on, don't be afraid to take a risk. You never know where it might lead.

"Five minutes?" Mike asks.

"Five minutes," I reply.

Omar raises his head when I re-enter the room. He shuffles on his feet and his dirty white dishdasha sways around his ankles. The goat snorts a greeting from the corner. I walk over to Omar and place my face close to his, our noses almost touching. His eyes grow wide.

"We have a problem," I say with a hard stare.

He shuffles on his feet.

"You lied to me," I say.

"I did not lie," Omar replies.

"Really? Then why does your brother say that you

have a relative named Abu Azir that lives near here that you never mentioned?"

Biggie raises his voice.

"I don't know an Abu Azir," Omar pleads.

"It's a lie," I say.

The scar below his eye twitches.

"I'm telling the truth!" he pleads.

"Your brother is smart enough not to lie, so why aren't you smart enough not to lie?"

He shuffles on his feet.

"You're both teachers. I don't understand. Why is his memory better?"

No answer. I put my mouth to the side of his head right next to his ear and lower my voice to a whisper.

"Look, I don't want to take you back to the prison. Who's going to take care of your family while we get this sorted out? Huh?"

Silence.

"I want to help you," I say. "I didn't come to Iraq to split up families. I'm not here for you. If I was here for you then I wouldn't be asking you questions. You'd already be in my vehicle. I can leave you here, but you've got to tell me about Abu Azir."

"I don't know any Abu Azir."

I turn my head to the side, close my eyes, and grind my teeth. I tap my fingers on the wall next to Omar's head. The goat snorts as Mike enters the room behind me.

"I've got it."

I turn around.

"The brother is going to take us to Abu Azir's house."

Biggie raises his bushy eyebrows. I turn to Omar and he shuffles his feet.

"You're coming with us," I say.

4

The Assyrian

June 10, 2006

ZAFAR
↑
?
↑
ABU AZIR
(WEAPONS DEALER)
↑
OMAR
(TWIN BROTHER)

Outside, it's a calm, dark night. The last of the raid team straggles into the conference room and takes their seats. As we wait for the commander, there's a steady flow of conversation and laughter. At the front of the room our intelligence officer, Jeff, makes his last corrections to the day's briefing. Jeff is a bald captain with an academic air—a perfect intel-type.

Mike and I sit in the front row. We appear ancient in this crowd. The soldiers are covered in ink and when they're not snatching terrorists, they listen to heavy metal on their iPods, play *Halo* and *Grand Theft Auto,* drink Red Bull, read *Maxim,* cuss, work out, and pull pranks. Two old-timers (in their early thirties) sit quietly in the back—the career men and future Senior NCOs.

The friendliest of the bunch is the First Sergeant, a short version of Mr. Clean. Every unit has a guy like our First Sergeant—the first to give you his gun should yours malfunction. When I arrived, he took one look at the antique AR-15 that my unit had issued me for my deployment (reservists get the leftovers) and immediately lent me one of the unit's M-4s, with laser sighting. He also lent me a monocle night-vision device versus the twin tubes that I had brought, an advantage for interrogations where at night a 'gator wants to observe his surroundings while maintaining "naked" eye contact with a detainee. The First Sergeant treats Mike and me as team members, not as attached guests. He realizes that the lives of his men hinge on the accuracy of the information we elicit.

Our unit commander is a tall, late-thirties man with a long face. Major Templeton is coming up on his lieutenant colonel board, a career infantry officer with several deployments under his belt. A big-name kill or capture would look nice on his promotion recommendation, but he has peers.

There's an informal competition among the raid teams in our task force and captures and kills are tracked for each unit's rotation. You can be sure that the commanders know the score at all times. These are, after all, adrenaline-driven overachievers, yet these elite officers are quiet professionals. There's no one I'd rather have clear a house before I enter.

Major Templeton strides into the room and the First Sergeant calls it to attention. We jump from our seats.

"Carry on, gentlemen," Templeton says and takes a seat at the front of the room next to Jeff.

Jeff taps on the laptop and a video appears on the wall through a projector. It's a teaser for the next mission.

The view is not clear, but we are looking out from a rooftop at a roundabout in downtown Kirkuk. The camera focuses and the roundabout comes into view. Heavy traffic moves erratically around the intersection, cars darting, honking, inching forward, and then stopping. The camera shakes and watching is a bit dizzying.

Suddenly an American convoy appears at the roundabout and stops, yielding to the traffic. The camera zooms in and we see that the front truck is a desert-colored half ton. There's a break in the traffic and the half ton pulls into the roundabout. As it makes its way around, a red sedan quickly enters the roundabout perpendicular to the half ton. Instantly, the scene erupts in smoke and flames. The camera shakes, trying to hold the scene in view, and then the screen goes black. This is Zafar's revenge for our most recent capture. Whispered condemnations fill the room.

Major Templeton shakes his head and gives Jeff a nod. A slide appears on the wall with a wire diagram of al Qaeda in northern Iraq. At the bottom of the diagram are names crossed off with X's—terrorists that the unit has captured or killed. All of the crossed-out names point to one name in the center of the slide—Abu Azir—and below his name in parenthesis is "weapons dealer." Above Abu Azir's name on the diagram is a question mark that points to a final name at the top of the slide: Zafar.

Jeff addresses us from his seat in front of the laptop. "Gentlemen, this is where we are. As you all know, last night we captured the twin brothers and they identified the house of Abu Azir, but we decided to call off the mission until we could confirm it through other sources."

The commander likes us 'gators, but he doesn't trust the information we extract until he can validate it. Waiting puts us at a serious disadvantage. Al Qaeda can adjust to their loss and Abu Azir might move if he believes the twin brothers would cooperate and give away his location. Jeff continues.

"Well, an hour ago I received a phone call from our confidential source. He confirmed the location of the house of Abu Azir. The source also says that Abu Azir carries a list on him with the names and addresses of the men in his cell. We need that list. We're launching sometime in the next few hours. Tonight's intel cards are here on the table. Pick one up on your way . . ."

The door opens and in walks a spook with an unkempt beard, long hair, and a black baseball cap. He wears Blades sunglasses even though it's dark outside. With his hands in his pockets, he nonchalantly approaches the major and whispers in his ear. The major's eyes light up.

"What do you mean, 'gone'?" Templeton asks.

The cat out of the bag, the spook speaks out loud, "AWOL, sir. He's gone AWOL."

Jeff turns from the laptop. "Mahmoud?"

The spook looks at Jeff and nods his head. The short chain on our terrorist turned undercover mole just broke.

*　　*　　*

The episode ends—another conspiracy, another run-in with the mayor, and another team member goes native. We're watching *The Shield: Season 1* in our makeshift office space, a plywood walled 20'×40' room. We sit on black ergonomic chairs behind our metal desks. We have $800 chairs, but neither Mike nor I have been able to get our hands on something that might save our lives—a radio headset that fits inside our helmets. The unit has no spares. We need a Milo Minderbinder.

We are partaking in the new American military pastime—watching DVDs. On my last deployment to Saudi Arabia, we went through every episode of *Friends* (it's boring in the desert). This time we plan to cover the first three seasons of *The Shield* and *Band of Brothers,* which I've already seen twice. When we are not interrogating our detainees or writing reports, we stare at a new seventy-two-inch plasma television mounted on the wall, waiting for the Bat Phone to ring. When it rings, about 99 percent of the time it's a call to meet at the Strykers for a mission. The lead time is ten minutes.

You grow accustomed to the schedule quickly, which means that you get used to complete randomness. There's no predictability as to when a target is developed and the decision is made that there is enough intelligence to launch. Sometimes we go at noon, sometimes at midnight, and sometimes at six in the morning, after you've been up all night interrogating and just lowered your head to your pillow. There are no days off. This is not a marathon; it is a full-out sprint.

Mike lifts the remote. The music starts for the next episode. Just as Mackey appears on screen and enters a smoky lounge full of Russian mafia, the Bat Phone rings.

Mike answers.

"Meet at the Strykers in ten minutes."

*   *   *

"Lock and load!" the TC yells toward the back.

We rack the slides on our weapons as the Stryker accelerates out the gate. We hum along route NEBRASKA. I look across at Mike and he's leaning back in repose, lost in thought. You wonder every once in a while, *What is everyone else thinking right now?* We all know the risks. This is my fourth war deployment and I have no apprehension. On the raid team, going outside the wire every day, sticking my head out of the porthole and scanning the rooftops, I feel free. After three and a half months conducting interrogations inside a prison and never leaving an enclosed compound, this is like swimming in the middle of the Pacific Ocean, and it's liberating. I just hope there are no sharks.

"Why are you grinning?" Mike yells across at me.

"No reason," I yell back.

I flip down my night-vision monocle and test my infrared laser designator on my rifle to ensure it works. Soon, they'll be calling for airguards. I checked it once before we left, but you can never be too sure with anything that runs on batteries. Sure thing, it's dead. I keep spare batteries in the arm pocket of my green uniform and I remove them and replace the dead ones. Still nothing. I check the wiring on the outside. Everything looks fine. I rotate the batteries one at a time. Nothing. I pull the device up to my face and inspect the contacts. They look good. And then sound evaporates.

The explosion is louder than a Kiss concert. The driver hits the brakes and we crush together in back. I look up and check the men around me. They're all wide-eyed.

"Everyone okay?" I yell.

No one can hear me, so I raise a thumb. Everyone nods or returns it. The TC yells, "Speed up!!! *Speed the fuck up!!!*"

I look to the front of the Stryker at the black and white television monitor that displays a live video feed of the road in front of us. The Stryker that we were following is gone. All that remains is a giant cloud of smoke.

Our driver hits the gas, the engine screams, we lurch forward, accelerate, and enter the cloud. We must be doing fifty miles an hour.

It needs no explanation what sixteen tons of metal would do to another sixteen tons of metal if they were to collide at our speed. We fly blindly through the smoke and, seconds later, emerge on the other side. Our sister Stryker is in front of us.

The radio is full of chatter as we continue toward our target—the house of Abu Azir—confirmed just an hour ago. The Stryker slows and we turn a corner. Mike and I look at each other and shake our heads. There are no reports of casualties in the other Stryker.

"Airguards!"

The last thing one wants to do after a roadside bomb goes off next to your vehicle is stick your head outside, but that's exactly what we do. Mike and I rise from our seats and pop open the rear hatches. I emerge into the warm night air, flip down my monocle, and begin scanning for targets. I remember the problem with my batteries and try my laser designator. It works. Go figure. I start scanning the rooftops and windows, looking for targets.

We are on a two-lane road bordering a middle-class neighborhood. On one side of the road are two-story homes; on the other side is desert. We slowly come to a stop next to a T intersection that leads into the neighborhood. I see soldiers disembark the Strykers ahead of us and begin trotting down the street.

" 'Gators!" the TC calls from the front.

Mike and I lower ourselves from the hatches as the rear door opens. We exit with Biggie and Tiny in trail and trot down the street after the soldiers. We run along a brick wall and I remember the words of our tactics instructor during pre-deployment training in Georgia: "Bullets hug walls." I leave space between me and the bricks.

The street is dark and silent. The team moves in unison quickly, quietly. It's a strange sensation running with one eye on night-vision and one eye naked, but the mind adapts and soon it's second nature.

We approach another intersection and turn left. The team is thirty yards ahead of us, crouched down in front of a brick wall that guards a row of three-story townhomes. I see the Alabama Lieutenant hovering with the First Sergeant over a map. Mike and I close the distance to ten yards and then kneel down and provide security for our rear flank. We put Biggie and Tiny behind us. They have body armor, but no weapons.

After less than a minute, half of the team moves again along the wall, turns, and disappears at the end of the row of townhomes. A soldier returns a short time later.

"Stay here until we call for you. The target house is in front of these townhomes."

I nod. The other half of the team moves out except for two soldiers who make their way to the three-story townhomes and scale a rear balcony like spiders. Within seconds they are on the roof.

I continue to scan the street in front. There's a brick wall a hundred yards in the distance. It's completely silent and not a dog is barking. That worries me.

Suddenly, I hear a small explosion followed by the echo of metal falling onto stone. A minute later a soldier reappears at the end of the row of townhomes and waves us forward.

I step through the front door and glass cracks beneath my boots. The doorway leads directly into a narrow staircase. Biggie barely fits. I flip up my night-vision monocle and we go up the stairs and emerge into a family room. A soldier is busy dumping out drawers from the entertainment center. He turns around, sees us, and points to the hallway.

Down the hallway I peer into a room and see the Alabama Lieutenant and another soldier standing next to an Iraqi in flannel pajamas. The Iraqi has his hands flexicuffed behind his back.

"The wife and kids are in the next room," the Lieutenant says.

I turn to Mike and the terps.

"Biggie and I will take this one," I say.

Mike nods and continues with Tiny to the next room. As I approach, the Lieutenant heads for the door. The other soldier starts to search the room—opening drawers, looking under the bed, and sifting through the closet. I stand in front of the captured Iraqi.

He is bald on top with black hair that flows around his neck from ear to ear. He wears round, gold-rimmed spectacles and is an inch shorter than my six feet.

"As-salamu alaykum," I say as I wipe the sweat from my forehead on the back of my glove.

"Alaykum as-salam," he replies in a soft voice, his eyes avoiding mine.

"What is your name?" I ask.

Before Biggie can translate he replies in English.

"Akram," he says.

"I'm pleased to meet you, Akram," I say.

He nods politely.

"I'm going to ask you some questions. It's very important that you are—"

"Is my family okay?" he interrupts.

"Yes, your family is fine."

He nods politely again, still avoiding eye contact.

"You can look at me," I say.

45

He glances up and then down again. His eyes are black as night.

"Who lives in this house?" I ask.

"Just me, my wife, and my children. I have one son and one daughter."

"What are the names of your children?"

This is important. We are looking for an Abu Azir and Abu means "father of." If his son's name is Azir . . . jackpot.

"Badi and Yasmin," he replies.

No luck.

"Has anyone visited your house recently or stayed here?"

"No, no one."

He sniffs. I inspect his face. He continues to avoid eye contact.

"Do you have any brothers?"

We run through the names of his relatives. No Abu Azir and no Azir. I run through his extended family. No dice.

The soldier in the room finishes his search and heads out the door.

"It's clean," he says on his way out.

"Thanks," I reply.

I focus on Akram.

"What is your job?" I ask.

"I am a banker."

"A banker? Where do you work?"

"I own a bank on the main plaza."

"How long have you been a banker?"

"All my life," he replies.

Akram glances up and then back down again.

"Are you sure my family is okay?" he asks.

"Yes," I say, "your family is fine."

My neck is stiff from the weight of my helmet and I roll it. As I glance around the room something strange catches my attention. There is a wooden cross on the wall. On the cross is a silver, crucified Jesus. Biggie, who has been standing silently next to me, has a look. We turn to each other with the same strange expression. I look at Akram.

"Are you Muslim?" I ask.

"No, we are Christians," Akram replies. "Assyrians."

Assyrians are an ancient people of the Fertile Crescent whose origins date back to the Akkadian Empire, circa 2300 B.C. They are some of the earliest Christians, converting between the first and third centuries. There are a million Assyrians in Iraq, about 3 percent of the population, yet almost half of them have fled the country—victims of al Qaeda persecution.

One of my Iraqi culture instructors during our tactical training course was a young Assyrian woman. She told me that Assyrians were protected under Saddam and that when she lived in Iraq she wore blue jeans and a gold cross around her neck and walked the streets of Baghdad without fear. No more.

I turn to Biggie. He nods his head—he believes Akram. Iraqis know these things intuitively.

"Are you afraid of living in Iraq right now?" I ask.

"Yes, I am," Akram replies. "I thought you were al Qaeda coming to kill us."

I reach inside the medical kit strapped to my belt and pull out surgical scissors. Akram attempts to back up but bumps into the dresser behind him.

"I'm just going to free your hands," I say.

He looks apprehensive as I reach around and cut his hands free. He immediately rubs at his wrists.

"Sorry about that," I say, "but we have to be careful."

"I understand," he says softly.

"Still, I need your help," I reply.

He stops rubbing his wrists.

"What are the names of your neighbors?" I ask.

"My neighbors?"

"Yes."

He looks at Biggie and then turns to me. "You are asking something very dangerous."

"I understand," I say, "but we need your help."

He lifts a hand and rubs his face.

THE ASSYRIAN

"You can tell people that we treated you poorly so that they won't know you cooperated," I say.

He continues to stroke his face.

"I can pay you," I say.

"I have money," he replies.

"What can I do for you?"

"I have everything I need," he says, "but it doesn't matter now. Even if I tell you nothing, no one will believe me. We must leave."

We've contaminated him with our presence.

"I'm sorry," I say. "It was an honest mistake."

He quits rubbing his face and rubs again at his wrists. "Who are you looking for?"

"Abu Azir," I reply.

"This is a very dangerous man," he says.

I don't reply. Sometimes silence is an interrogator's best weapon. Ten seconds pass. Twenty. Akram inspects my face and contemplates. Finally, he exhales and speaks:

"Three houses down on the left."

Two minutes later the entire raid team is lined up in front of the house three doors down. There's a black steel gate and in a split second a soldier pulls bolt cutters from his backpack and snaps the chain. The soldiers rush into the courtyard. They kick in the front door, rush through,

49

and capture Abu Azir sleeping on the living room floor next to his daughter, two sons, and wife, without a shot fired.

He is not scared. Abu Azir leans with his back against the wall in the living room, his hands fastened behind him. His white dishdasha is stained and wrinkled, and rises and falls on his portly midsection. I raise the monocle from my eye. He has thick, gray-streaked hair and a rough beard. With steady eyes he studies my face. Biggie is at my side, tapping his foot.

"*As-salamu alaykum,*" I say.

He doesn't reply. I take his silence as surprise so I repeat myself.

"*As-salamu alaykum.*"

He looks down and answers.

"*Alaykum as-salam.*"

Biggie knows my routine and doesn't try to assist my poor Arabic.

"*Kayfa halek?*" I ask.

"Okay, okay," Abu Azir answers without looking up.

"Don't worry about your family. We are not going to hurt them."

Abu Azir looks up from the floor. He grunts and exhales.

Mike is in the next room questioning Abu Azir's wife

while soldiers search through the house around us—upending furniture and spilling the contents of drawers onto the stone floor, covering it in clothes, pictures, papers, and keepsakes. The house was a well-kept middle-class home before the soldiers started in on it. Slowly, they begin to find weapons and haul them out of the house. First they find rifles. Then a machine gun. Then blasting caps. Then grenades. The soldiers find the weapons in the cupboard, the entertainment center, the closet, the oven, the garage, and under the sofa next to where Abu Azir was sleeping with his kids. They pull ammunition from the drawers of the end tables. It's like Rambo's Easter Egg Hunt. I turn to Abu Azir.

"I know what you're thinking. You're thinking that you're going to say that you don't know anything."

While Biggie translates, Abu Azir stares at me.

"You are thinking that you can get out of this. Maybe you have a plan, but, rest assured, there are two things that are certain."

I pause to let Biggie convey my words. Biggie's arm brushes up against me as he raises two fingers in the air.

"The first thing is that you have to make a decision. If you decide to do nothing, that is a decision."

I pause.

"The second thing is that if you help me, then I will help you. I have to do so according to our custom. You

51

and me, we have to answer to the same God, and I will not lie. If I say I will help you, I will help you."

As Biggie translates, Abu Azir looks down at the floor again and shuffles on his feet.

"You know why we're here. You know who we are looking for."

The dishdasha sways at Abu Azir's feet while he shifts his weight from one foot to the other. There are tiny movements of the muscles around his eyes.

This is the start of the futility approach. Both U.S. Army interrogators and detectives are taught this same technique. You present a detainee with overwhelming evidence, laying it all out before them. You don't give them a chance to object, starting with the assumption that you are already past the admission of guilt phase. Now you're just working on the deal.

"I understand why you are involved," I continue. "This is the only way for Sunnis to survive."

The first time I said these words, Biggie, being a Shi'a, struggled with them. This time they flow quickly. He understands the game.

"We are not here to harm Iraqis. We are looking for foreigners. The Sunnis fighting with the Shi'a is none of our business. In fact, I might be able to help you."

I take off my helmet and hold it next to my body. I can feel the rolling beads of sweat on my forehead. I decide to use a ruse. I'll ask him if he knows a fictional "foreigner." It will allow me to gauge his mannerisms and at the same time probe how willing he is to cooperate.

"You tell me where to find the foreigner and I'll take care of you. Do you know which foreigner I am talking about?"

"I don't know any foreigners."

He says it without emotion, looking straight into my eyes.

"Why would my source tell me that you have met with the foreigner twice in the last week?"

He blinks at the word "twice."

"Do you think I would come here in the middle of the night with all these soldiers and create this mess if I wasn't certain that you knew the foreigner? There are a lot of bombs on the roads these days. I wouldn't take that risk if I wasn't certain. My source also said you would work with us, that you are a good man who wants to help Sunnis, and take care of his family."

As Biggie translates, Abu Azir shuffles on his feet again. I'm now mixing in another approach, Love of Family, and using culture as leverage. As a good Muslim he is obligated to provide for his family. This is an orchestra of approaches—the new way of interrogating.

"I want to help you, but I don't know any foreigners," he says.

"Where's the list?"

He stops shuffling. I use surprise because he's too composed. I need to disrupt his mental confidence.

"I don't know what you are talking about," Abu Azir answers.

"I know about the list. I know it's here, in the house. Look, I don't want to damage your house and I don't want to question your wife and children. I didn't come to Iraq to cause trouble for Iraqis. I came here only to find the foreigners. If you care about your family and your home, like a good Muslim, then you will tell me the location of the list."

"I don't know about any list."

I look at Biggie and his face is stuck in a scowl. He is disgusted by these Sunnis involved in the insurgency. One only has to look at the television on any given day to see Shi'a bodies littering the streets. I've wondered if Biggie thinks of the Sunni bodies.

"Look, my friend"—I put my hand on Abu Azir's shoulder and take a step toward him—"I want to help you. I don't want to take you back to the base. Who's going to look after your family?"

He is still.

"Your oldest son is how old? Ten?"

"Twelve."

"Twelve years old. Can he work, make money, and support your family while you are in prison?"

"No."

"I don't want that to happen. I can protect you. Hell, I'll say that you never told me anything and that my source gave me the information. Let's work together. I have nothing against Sunnis. I just want to find the foreigner, and his name and address are on your list."

"I don't know about a list."

As Biggie translates the words he shakes his massive head. He continues to scowl at Abu Azir.

Interrogations are unpredictable. Sometimes you use all the tools in your tool bag and none of them work. You can run the perfect approach, but that only increases the probability for success. A detainee might refuse to cooperate despite the quality of the interrogator's technique. Yet there's always an element of the unknown in dealing with human behavior. I believe I'm using the correct approach, but I could be wrong.

My information on Abu Azir is good. According to Jeff it was confirmed through a reliable source other than Mahmoud. There's a list in the house.

The Alabama Lieutenant approaches and pats me on the back, our signal for a private conversation. I leave Abu Azir with Biggie and step into the living room. I trust Biggie, but I keep an eye on him through the doorway.

"Zafar was planning something big," the Lieutenant says. "You see all this stuff?"

"It's a damn arms factory," I reply.

"Do you have anything?" he asks.

"Not yet, but I'm just getting started. Have your guys found anything?"

"We found ten thousand dollars upstairs under the mattress in the bedroom, but no list."

I look around the living room. The floor is covered in personal effects.

"Alright," the Lieutenant says, "let me know if you get something. As usual, we don't want to be here too long."

Abu Azir stares at his feet and Biggie rests with his back against the wall. I walk over to Abu Azir and stand face-to-face. It's time to up the ante.

"Look, we don't have much time. The General back at the base is angry. He says you have to make a decision. If you want me to help you, you've got to give me the list now."

He listens to my words and wets his lips with his tongue. His broad forehead is covered in sweat. I'm now using *wasta*, the Arabic word for power and influence. This is another way of leveraging culture. I'm using a fictitious relationship to a General back at the base to build my own *wasta* and, hence, my ability to help Abu Azir if he decides to cooperate. I learned this trick while stationed in Saudi Arabia, where I often had to leverage my relationship with an air force wing commander to get the Saudi security and intelligence services to act.

"I don't know about a list," Abu Azir says.

"Okay, don't say I didn't try to help you."

I leave Abu Azir with Biggie and walk to the next room where Mike is questioning Abu Azir's wife. When I enter, he turns from his kneeling position. Abu Azir's wife sits on the floor in front of him wearing a black burkha with only her face exposed. Three children, two boys and a girl, sit next to her on the floor. They are silent and still, staring at our foreign faces and the rifles hanging from our vests, always fixed to our hands.

"Anything?" I ask.

"No," Mike says. "She says no one's been at the house in a week except for her sister. And she says she's never seen a list."

"Can I talk to you for a second outside?"

"Sure."

We step outside the house into the courtyard and stand on broken glass in front of the metal door, which lies on stone at the entrance. There's a soldier posted at the gate, scanning the street.

"I think one of the kids has the list," Mike says.

"What makes you think that?" I ask.

"One of the soldiers told me that they were all sleeping together on the floor of the living room when he entered.

If the list was on Abu Azir when we arrived, then he could easily have slipped it to one of the kids before they got to him. The source says he carries it on him, but they already searched him and found nothing."

"But we can't search kids," I reply.

"I know," Mike says.

There is no official policy about searching kids on the battlefield and it never came up in our training. We're in no-man's-land. In these situations, you use your best judgment, but we can't create more enemies than we capture. It would be counterproductive.

I kick at some broken glass at my feet and Mike looks around the courtyard, scratching at his short-trimmed beard. The blue of his eyes is visible in the dark.

"I have an idea," he says.

"Go ahead."

"What if we get Abu Azir to give an order to the kids to give him the list?"

"Do you think he'll do that?" I ask.

"If he refuses to give the order, then at least we know for sure that the list is on one of the kids."

How am I going to convince Abu Azir to give the order? Maybe he'll just do it if I tell him to. There's a lesson I learned in psychology class about human behavior. People defer to those in positions of authority, even when it is illogical. This will be my own private Milgram experiment.

The children stand in a line in the living room from oldest to youngest; their mother sits behind them on the couch. The oldest child is a slender girl with light brown hair. She wears a white cotton dress and appears unusually calm. Her two black-haired brothers stand next to her, constantly turning to their mother for reassurance. I turn Abu Azir around to face his children.

"Okay, just as we discussed," I say through Biggie.

At the sight of his children, Abu Azir's face cracks for the first time. His eyes fill with water and a tear rolls down his cheek. He quickly turns his head to his shoulder and wipes it on his dishdasha, leaving a smear. This is the Love of Family approach like I've never run it before.

Abu Azir collects himself, shuffles on his feet, sticks out his chest as best he can over his potbelly, and lets out a rush of air. The seconds feel like lifetimes. He looks at each of the faces of his children, and then at his wife. Finally, he hangs his head. And then the Arabic flows from his mouth.

"Children, give to me what you are hiding."

Before the sentence is finished, his daughter's hand reaches under her white cotton dress. She pulls out a narrow roll of paper, takes a step forward, and holds it proudly in front of her father, a smile on her face. I take it from her hand as Abu Azir grunts.

The Alabama Lieutenant leans over my shoulder to look at the roll of paper. "These are the addresses?"

I unroll the paper. The list is in Arabic.

"Yes," Biggie says.

"Hot damn!" the Lieutenant says. "Let's load up. We're going back to the base."

He taps team members on the back and they retreat from the house to our caravan in the street. Mike grabs Abu Azir and heads for the Stryker. I pull the Lieutenant to the side.

"About the family," I say. "Abu Azir isn't coming back for a long time."

"You can say that again," the Lieutenant answers. "Did you see all the shit we pulled out of this place?"

"We could leave his wife some of the cash you found upstairs," I suggest, "to take care of the kids."

The Lieutenant turns and looks at Abu Azir's wife. She sits on the couch with her children, the youngest boy cradled in her arms. Tears streak down her face as she rocks the child. I can't imagine the stress and worry she's been through anticipating this moment, knowing full well the danger her husband was exposing them to with his arms dealing. Here are the victims of war, in the flesh. And they exist on both sides.

"Okay, we'll leave her the cash," the Lieutenant agrees.

"All of it?" I ask.

"Yes, all of it."

* * *

The Stryker is parked in the center of the maintenance garage. A mechanic rolls underneath on a dolly.

"Control arm is bent," he says.

"How long to fix it?" the Alabama Lieutenant asks.

"A few hours," the mechanic replies.

I kneel down and stick my hand through a hole. The Stryker's rims look like Swiss cheese and four of the eight tires are shredded to pieces. The shrapnel from the IED—Improvised Explosive Device—passed through the steel as if it were warm butter.

"Pitch came in below the strike zone," Mike says.

"Close call," I reply.

"Another foot higher and it could have been bad," the Lieutenant says.

The culprit who planted the IED was a protégé of Iranian intelligence. Whoever planted it must have links to Iraq's old archenemy. Next time, we might not be so lucky.

5

Chasing Ghosts

*A person who does not speak out against the wrong is a
mute devil.* —ARAB PROVERB

June 12, 2006

B ack in our office, Mike and I remove our tactical gear
and place it in our wall bins. You don't fully realize
the weight of your equipment until you remove it, especially the body armor. Jeff opens the door and enters.

"I heard the news," Jeff says. "Zafar must have been
planning a big attack."

"It's only a matter of time before he regroups," Mike
replies.

"I understand you guys played a little trick on Abu
Azir," Jeff says.

"Who would have thought that would work?" I answer.

Mike shakes his head.

"Unbelievable," he says.

"We can get more information from Abu Azir," I say
to Jeff. "We'll go in with him tonight."

"No need," Jeff says. "He's on his way to the main prison."

Damn. I wanted another shot at him before he left, but some of our catches are directly linked to terrorists on target sets in other parts of the country. We have to be team players.

Biggie knocks and enters the room.

"I asked him to help with the list," Jeff says. "Mind if we go over it together?"

"Let's do it," I say.

We clear our weapons, stow them in our bins, and then sit down at a desk. Jeff pulls out the list and the four of us hover over it.

It's a long, thin piece of paper, a grocery list of terrorists—but instead of milk and eggs, there are names and addresses. Jeff counts down the list.

". . . nine, ten, eleven. Eleven new targets!"

"Yeah," I say, "but which of these lead up the ladder and which lead down?"

Biggie suddenly puts his finger next to a name on the list. "Zafar!"

We look at each other with wide eyes.

"There could be more than one Zafar," Jeff says, his voice filled with caution.

We return to the list.

"Wait, wait . . ." Biggie says. "Zafar's address looks familiar."

He reflects for a moment, searching his memories. Biggie has been in Iraq for two years working as an interpreter. He's been to hundreds of homes.

"This address is an old neighborhood in the suburbs," he says. "Mansoor Street, number twenty-five."

"Holy shit!" Jeff shouts. "That's Mahmoud's address!"

"Mahmoud?" I ask. "Zafar lives with Mahmoud?"

A split second of silence is interrupted by four simultaneous lightbulbs.

"Son of a bitch!" Mike says, shaking his head.

"You've got to be kidding me," I reply.

Jeff says what everyone's thinking.

"Mahmoud is Zafar."

Son of a bitch.

"We had him," I reply, "and let him go."

* * *

Jeff explains to a full conference room that Mahmoud and Zafar are the same guy. As soon as he says it, a flurry of curses fills the room. It's one thing for young men to risk their lives night after night to capture these men behind the suicide bombings. It's another for them to risk their lives to go after a guy we already had and let go.

This age-old lesson of counterinsurgency is not an easy one to swallow. We know that what we're doing is complicated—and it's about to get worse.

"Quiet," Major Templeton orders from the front of the room. "Let Jeff finish."

The room falls silent.

"There is a silver lining," Jeff says. "One of the names on the list we already know. It's a guy named Hamza. He's a truck driver that ferries weapons from Iran to Iraq. We think he works for a guy named Walid, a member of Ansar al-Islam. Al Qaeda and Ansar al-Islam are working hand in hand."

It's a promising lead and the strategy is clear: Find Hamza, get him to give us Walid, and then get Walid and convince him to lead us to Mahmoud—always working up the ladder. Jeff continues.

"However, we've already been by the house and his truck is not there. He must be making a weapons run. As soon as the truck reappears at the address on this list we took from Abu Azir, we'll hit it."

Optimistic whispers race around the room.

"Until then," Major Templeton says, standing up, "we're going after the other targets on the list."

He turns to Jeff.

"Give them the first target," Templeton says. "We start tonight."

I started playing soccer when I was seven, on the same team as my brother. My father was the assistant coach. The strategy of the game appeals to me. I remember my uncle, my father's older brother, telling me when I was young, "Soccer is a thinking man's sport. It's all about strategy."

I follow the American men's national soccer team, but it's frustrating. They have moments of pure brilliance, at times playing to the level of powerhouses like Brazil, Germany, and Italy, and then they fall to tiny third world countries that most fans couldn't locate on a map. This year they seem ripe for success as the World Cup gets under way in Germany.

Mike isn't a soccer fan, but he agrees to watch the first game—the United States versus the Czech Republic. The Czechs have a solid squad and it will be a test. I'm concerned that we won't get through the game without the Bat Phone ringing.

Two hours later I sit dejected in my seat.

"Well, better luck next game," Mike says. "I have to say, though, I enjoyed it."

The United States effort was lackluster and they went with a strategy that I abhor, playing not to lose, instead of to win. Their lack of confidence irritates me and I blame the coaching.

"Three to zilch," Mike says. "Not very impressive."

I shake my head.

"You miss a hundred percent of the shots you don't take," I reply.

"Exactly," Mike says, "but on the other side of the coin, you can't shoot just for the sake of taking shots."

The metaphor isn't lost on me. Rumors are circulating within the unit that Templeton wants results. He's behind in the polls compared to the other commanders in Iraq— less captures, less kills. The recent focus has been on Baghdad, especially in the aftermath of Zarqawi's death. The intel gleaned from that operation gave the teams in central Iraq enough fodder to last a month. They conduct one raid after another, but in the grand scheme of things, it's all down the ladder. The man who took Zarqawi's place, Abu Ayyub al-Masri, the Egyptian, is said to have fled Iraq. Al Qaeda has accepted defeat in Baghdad. The Shi'a militias have a stranglehold on the capital.

After the last intel brief, Jeff told Mike and me that in Anbar Province, specifically Ramadi, the marines are negotiating with the Sunni sheikhs. Some marine and army company-grade officers believe they can peel the Sunnis back from al Qaeda with money and weapons; the first inroads to this strategy are being tested. Meanwhile al Qaeda, bracing for the worst, continues to move north, directly into our line of fire.

The Bat Phone rings and Mike answers it.

"Yes. Okay."

He puts down the phone.

"Ten minutes," he says.

"Here we go again," I reply.

———

"Lock and load!" the TC yells.

We rack our rifles as we exit the back gate and roll down route FLORIDA toward our target. There have been more roadside bombs on route FLORIDA than any other road in Kirkuk.

There was no rhyme or reason to the names on the list other than the Hamza-Walid-Mahmoud connection, so Jeff picked the first name on the list. We're going to try and stir up the pot and see what floats to the top. The first name on the list was Haitham; the address directs us to one of Kirkuk's poorest neighborhoods—a shantytown of cinder-block homes with crude tin roofs.

The back of the Stryker is boiling, the sun directly overhead. It's our first day mission since my arrival. We drink furiously from the CamelBaks strapped to our backs. By the time they call for airguards ten minutes later, I can already feel sweat puddles collecting in the bottoms of my boots.

I push open the hatch and a relief of wind hits my face. I emerge from the hole and take in my surroundings. We're on a narrow two-lane road; to my left is the shantytown. Up ahead is a T-intersection, the crossroad leading into the neighborhood. Cars pass in the opposite direction. It's been a long time since I've seen Iraqis on the streets.

As we turn into the neighborhood, a chicken crosses the road in front of us while two young boys stand next to a cinder-block house, playing with sticks in the dirt. They stare as we pass. One of them waves and I wave in return. In my other hand, my M-4 rests against the top of the Stryker.

The medics below have radios and headsets inside their helmets to monitor the communications traffic. The radio crackles below and I hear a muffled conversation.

"Any idea what they are saying?" I shout to Mike, who is sticking outside the porthole beside me, scanning for targets on the opposite side. Our request to headquarters for headsets has fallen on deaf ears, so we're still unable to listen to the team's internal communications.

"No clue," Mike shouts.

Suddenly, the formation stops. A few men emerge from their houses to observe. They smoke cigarettes and scratch at their beards. None of them appears intimidated by the armored green beasts that have taken up residence in the middle of their neighborhood. The radio below continues to crackle, then the formation starts up again. The lead vehicle quickly accelerates and makes a massive, sweeping U-turn. It rolls through the dirt yard in front of a house before heading in the opposite direction. Our line of baby ducks follows suit.

Our formation accelerates to fifty miles an hour on the two-lane road that led us into the shantytown.

We return to route FLORIDA, a six-lane highway. I take a second to squat down in the porthole and yell to the medic next to me, "Any word on where we are going?"

The medic looks up at me and yells back, "Someone says the target left the house in a white truck just before we arrived! We're chasing him!"

I rise back up through the porthole. Our formation is racing down the highway, weaving in and out of traffic. I yell over at Mike, "Why do we still have airguards?"

"I have no idea!" he yells back.

It's one of those insane things about being a soldier. We follow orders even when it doesn't make sense. I'm okay with that. Mike calls it necessary "ass pain." I can't disagree, but I feel a responsibility for Mike and the terps. Mike can handle himself and has the composure of a much more seasoned veteran, the result of his time as a cop, but he's still new to the military and needs my advice on navigating the culture from time to time. That said, I never forget my responsibilities as the higher ranking officer. My inclination is to yell at the medic and have him radio the command vehicle to ask if we still need airguards. Suddenly, the driver slams on the brakes—traffic jam.

The scene quickly becomes comical. Our pack of Strykers wrapped in steel cages (protection from RPGs) is at a virtual standstill in Kirkuk's rush hour. An instinct arises in me to lay on the horn, but Strykers don't have horns, although the manufacturer may want to consider those in the next modification.

"You gotta hate commuting to work through rush hour traffic!" Mike yells.

I inspect the cars pulling up alongside. The Iraqis spare us no space—it's just another typical day. Next to us is a seventies-era blue Datsun hatchback, just like my first car. I spent much of my adolescence driving that car to and from the beach with my surfboard in back.

Behind the wheel of the blue Datsun is a man about my age in a white dishdasha. He has curly black hair and a short black beard. His forehead is drenched in sweat, just like mine. He shakes his head and pokes it out the open window, peering around the cars to see what's holding up traffic. Ahead of us is a pedestrian bridge. As far as I can see, there is no reason for the jam.

The man in the Datsun looks up at me and we lock eyes, except I'm wearing sunglasses. The shatter resistant lenses are a must where roadside bombs are a threat. I nod at him and he nods back and smiles. In a sign to me, he throws his hand in the air indicating his helplessness in the clogged traffic. I smile and nod again. He smiles.

It's my first interaction with an Iraqi outside of an interrogation setting, not counting my Shi'a interpreters, and I want to sit down with this man. I want to share a cup of tea and ask questions.

I've learned enough about Sunnis in Iraq from my previous three and a half months of interrogations to fill a collection of encyclopedias, but I want to sit down with a Sunni outside of an interrogation booth. Just once I want to talk to a Sunni when I'm not holding a weapon, or he's not in an orange jumpsuit. In the prison there were men I interrogated who leveled with me. I remember one Sunni in particular who joined al Qaeda, only to be accused of being a mole, tortured, and then rescued by American forces. He told me everything he knew about al Qaeda and listed twenty homes where his cell members lived near Fallujah. I couldn't write the targets down fast enough as he called them off. I thought my pen might run out of ink. The problem was that he didn't know where the leader of his cell lived and I was only concerned with working up the ladder, not down.

Still, he told me of his frustration with America's policies in Iraq that put Sunnis out of work and let Shi'a militias run free. He told me that his son had been shot and killed in a gunfight between American forces and insurgents in Fallujah. He said that it had been an accident and he bore no grudge against Americans for the death of his son, but we both knew it was a lie. Now we shared a common enemy—the foreign al Qaeda members who were using Iraqis as tools for their extreme version of Islam and for a campaign of violence against innocent civilians. I heard similar stories from many Sunnis in Iraq. They didn't hate our way of life, they hated our policies in the Middle East. If we had met in a café in Europe we would have shared many views of the world, even if we'd never agree about a solution to the Israeli-Palestinian conflict. Or maybe we could find a compromise.

The Stryker slowly moves forward and as we make our way ahead of the blue Datsun, the driver waves good-bye to me. I nod in return.

Our formation cuts through the traffic to the shoulder and accelerates past the traffic jam with four wheels in the sand. At the pedestrian overpass, we finally discover the cause of the traffic jam: a broken sofa frame sits in the road, blocking two lanes.

Free of the jam, our formation picks up speed again. Ancient Japanese vehicles keep pace with our green monsters. A few minutes later we approach downtown and turn on to a two-lane road toward the center. We drive into a neighborhood of three-story dwellings, the bottom floors serving as shops. Our formation brings with it a tumultuous roar of engines, but rarely do the Iraqis bother to look, going about their business as if we are an everyday occurrence. They must think us a conventional forces patrol, not a kill or capture mission.

Below I hear the muffle of radio traffic again. The medic pulls on my pant leg and yells at me, "They're looking for a white truck!"

I stick a thumbs-up below and turn to Mike. "The medic says we're looking for a white truck. See any?"

"None on my side!" he yells back.

"Never played car chase in Iraq before," I say.

"Yeah, I don't like the looks of this," he replies.

"Maybe we can stop at the market and pick up some souvenirs."

"I want to get a T-shirt for my little girl," he says.

"I was thinking a tea set for my mother and a hookah pipe for my cousin," I reply.

We find ourselves almost at a stop again, trying to wedge between snack carts on the sides of the road. One of the vendors has to shoo away his customers and move his cart off the road so we can pass. We drive by the edge of a busy market and I peer into a fabric store. Two men in dishdashas are sitting on the floor drinking tea.

We are extremely vulnerable, a crunched formation of military vehicles barely able to crawl forward in this densely populated area. Tall buildings with flat roofs and balconies surround us. I remember the scene in the movie *Clear and Present Danger* where Harrison Ford's convoy of Suburbans gets trapped in a dense city block of tall buildings in Bogotá and is obliterated by terrorists.

The radio traffic below grows louder. There must be frustration in the command vehicle. Someone is yelling to get us out of here.

Twenty minutes later, as difficult as it was to drive into the downtown congestion, we drive out. A few turns and we find ourselves back on the two-lane road leading to the highway. We accelerate, swerve, and stop. And then absolute chaos ensues.

Four cars are stopped at the side of the road. The lead Stryker in our formation cut them off, trapping all four inside our formation. Soldiers are pulling men out of the cars and placing them facedown on the road.

The medic grabs my leg again and shouts, " 'Gators!"

Mike and I lower ourselves and run out the open ramp into the street with Biggie and Tiny behind us. I run to the closest vehicle, a white Suburban. Eight men are on the ground, facedown on the hot asphalt with their hands flexi-cuffed behind their backs. They are dressed in slacks and button-up shirts. Their pocket litter is strewn on the street beside them.

I find the Alabama Lieutenant red-faced and out of breath.

"Talk to these guys on the ground next to the Suburban," he says. "The other ones we're letting go."

"Did they leave the house?" I ask.

He wipes at his sweaty forehead. "To tell you the truth, I don't know."

Mike and I split up and Biggie comes with me. I pick out the oldest man in the group and kneel down beside him in the street. He has peppered black hair combed back on his head and a neatly trimmed mustache. He grimaces and tries to relieve the pressure on his shoulders by rotating them.

"What's your name?" I ask.

Biggie translates and the Iraqi turns and looks at me. He speaks in Arabic and Biggie repeats in English.

"My name is Ali. Why did you stop us? We didn't do anything."

"Where were you before here?" I ask.

"We were at a business meeting downtown!"

"What kind of business?"

"Clothes! We own clothing stores!"

"Where do you live?" I ask.

"In the downtown area!" he answers.

His face is red and he rolls his shoulders again.

The Alabama Lieutenant approaches me. "We're taking them back to the base. I don't want to hang out here in the open. One of my guys will drive the Suburban and follow us. Put two guys in your Stryker and we'll take the rest."

"Sure thing," I say.

Biggie helps raise the man to his feet. Mike and Tiny approach with another man and join us. Mike leans over and whispers to me, "Did your guy say they just came from a business meeting downtown?"

"Yes," I reply.

"I don't know about you . . ."

"I know," I interrupt. "This is starting to look like a complete cluster."

We pull back into our compound and park the Strykers

and the Suburban. I jump out the back of the vehicle and approach the Alabama Lieutenant.

"You got a second?" I ask.

"Sure, let's go over here," he replies.

We walk away from the line of men disembarking. Everyone is soaking wet from their heads to their toes. It feels like it's two thousand degrees.

"Why did we stop these guys?" I ask after we are out of earshot.

"We were looking for a white truck that left the house right before we arrived," he says.

"A white truck or a white Suburban?"

"They said a white truck but we had a communication problem."

"Can we call and find out?" I ask.

"Trust me, I already asked," the Lieutenant replies. "All they said is a white truck and then they gave us a last known location. Sorry, I wish I could tell you more."

"No problem," I say. "We'll figure it out."

The eight men are lined up in our holding area. It's a simple room of plywood walls and a concrete floor. Biggie instructs them not to talk. They are dressed like upper-class Iraqis—expensive leather shoes, slacks and button-up shirts, shiny gold watches, and neatly trimmed mustaches. In their manner of speech they are articulate and thoughtful.

One by one Mike and I question the men, asking the

same list of questions: Where were you before you were stopped? What were you doing? What is your business? Where do you live? Who are the other men with you? All of their stories match without a single discrepancy. We return the last man to the holding area and leave the group under the watchful eyes of the guards. The Doc has already checked them for injuries. Mike and I and the terps gather in the Doc's office next to the holding room.

"What do you think?" I ask.

"Their stories match," Mike says.

"These guys are just businessmen," Tiny says.

Tiny is barely five feet and a half. Back in the States he owns a computer store. He is a Shi'a Iraqi born in the south, and a father of six. He's one of our best terps. Always eager to help, no attitude.

"Biggie, what do you think?" I ask.

"I agree," he says. "They are businessmen. Why did we pull them over?"

"The Lieutenant said that a white truck left the house right before we got there," I reply.

"A white truck or a white Suburban?" Mike asks.

"That's exactly what I asked," I reply, "and he said he didn't know. Something about a communication problem."

Mike shakes his head.

"They are going to be pissed," Tiny says.

"Can we give them some money?" I ask Mike.

"There's a stash in the drawer of my desk. We confiscated it in a raid last month."

"Let's give them some money when we release them," I say. "I'll go talk to the major."

In the command post, Major Templeton is on the phone, sitting behind a computer. "Yes, sir. Got it."

He hangs up the phone.

"What you got?" he asks.

"Nothing," I reply. "We questioned each of the men separately and their stories match. They came from a business meeting downtown, not the target house."

"Okay, let them go."

"I'm going to give them some money," I say.

"Sure," he says and turns back to the computer.

I leave the command post and walk outside under the hot sun. I cross the compound toward our office and see the eight men tucking their shirts in and brushing the dirt off their pants as they pile back into the Suburban. Mike hands the driver a roll of cash and then gets into our SUV with Tiny. He drives toward the gate with the Suburban following close behind. My feet squish in my sweat-filled boots as I make my way toward my trailer. A cold shower suddenly seems like a great idea.

Freshly showered with five hours of sleep and a clean set of ACUs (Army Combat Uniform), I settle into my expensive ergonomic chair and turn on the flat-screen television. South Korea is beating Togo, 2–1. Mike enters the office and sits down at his desk behind me. He's also showered and wearing a clean set of ACUs.

"More soccer?" he says.

"I can turn it off if you want," I reply.

"It's kinda growing on me," he says.

We watch the last two minutes of the game and the Koreans hold on for a win. I mute the television.

"That was a bit of a cluster today, no?" I say.

"That was a total cluster," Mike replies.

The Bat Phone rings and Mike answers.

"Yes, sir. Got it."

Mike hangs up the phone.

"Let me guess, Stryker in ten minutes," I say.

"You got it."

Standing out the top of the Stryker, I scan for targets as we pull back into the shanty neighborhood of crumbling cinder-block homes we'd rumbled through just hours ago. The sun is low on the horizon, but the air still feels like a furnace on my face. I'm already soaked again with sweat.

Our formation zigzags into the neighborhood through the dirt streets; dogs run alongside and bark. Suddenly, the formation stops and soldiers pour out the backs of the vehicles. In seconds they are set up on the only two-story house in the shantytown. Snipers take up positions faster than a blink of an eye and men form a line next to the front door. In an instant, they kick in the door and rush inside. The medic pulls on my pant leg from below.

I exit the Stryker with Mike, the terps directly behind us. Before I can take three steps, however, a group of soldiers runs past me in the opposite direction. I stop and look for the Lieutenant. He's nowhere in sight.

Another small group of soldiers passes us in the street, runs to a house directly opposite the first house, and bursts through the front door. Meanwhile, the other group enters a house down the street. The Lieutenant appears from inside the first house and trots down the street with two soldiers behind him. The team is now scattered throughout three houses. I turn to Mike.

"Looks like a block party," I say.

"Maybe we should wait next to the Stryker," he replies.

"Good idea."

We return to the Stryker, watching the team take down houses. Half an hour later, they've gone through five homes and bring seven men back to the first house. The Lieutenant approaches me.

"Damn, it's hot," he says, wiping at his sweaty forehead. "You guys ready?"

"Yes," I reply. "Any weapons or paraphernalia in any of the homes?"

"No, nothing yet. We're still looking."

Mike and I and the terps walk over to the group of seven men sitting on the ground in an enclosed, cinder-block–walled courtyard. The men have their hands flexi-cuffed behind their backs. I choose the oldest of the group, a fifty-something-year-old man in a white dishda-sha. Mike grabs the youngest of the group, a man of about twenty in a sweat suit. I take my man inside the house with Biggie and put him up against the wall in the living room. I pull a bottle of water from a cargo pocket and offer it to him. He nods and I pour it into his mouth. After he swallows, I start.

"Is this your house?" I ask.

Biggie translates.

"Yes," he replies.

"What's your name?"

"Abu Bakr."

"Ah," I say, "you have a very respectful name. Abu Bakr was a disciple of Muhammad, Peace Be Upon Him."

As Biggie converts my words, Abu Bakr tilts his head.

"Are you Muslim?" he asks.

"No," I say, "but I've read the Quran."

Abu Bakr nods in approval.

"What is your work?" I ask.

"Please, look in my front pocket," he says.

I'm hesitant to do so. As a former criminal investiga-tor, I learned never to reach into a pocket—there could be a needle. Instead, I pat the pocket on the front of his white dishdasha with the back of my hand. I feel a wallet.

"What's in there?" I ask.

"My identification," he says.

I carefully open the top of the pocket and see that indeed there is a wallet inside. I remove and open it. On one side of the bifold is a police badge; on the other is his identification card. Abu Bakr says something to Biggie.

"He says that he is the police chief," Biggie says.

The identification is in Arabic so I show it to Biggie.

"It says he is the chief of police," he says after he inspects it.

"Could it be fake?" I ask.

Biggie looks around the room and inspects a clock on the wall.

"He's Shi'a," Biggie says.

"How do you know?" I ask.

"The clock on the wall. See the painting on the face?"

I look at the clock face. The painting is a landscape with some Arabic writing on it. For me, it's a mystery, but Biggie knows instantly.

"Only a Shi'a would have that clock in his house," Biggie says.

I inspect Abu Bakr's badge and credentials again. I see no reason to suspect they are counterfeit.

"Do you have any weapons in the house?" I ask.

"No, I don't keep guns here," he says. "No one knows I am the chief of police."

"What do you mean?" I ask.

Biggie translates and then turns to me. "He says that it is a secret. If people find out, he will be killed."

"What is the address of this house?" I ask.

"Number seventy-two," he says.

I pull my notepad out of my vest and check again the target address that Jeff gave to us before the mission. It's number eighty-two. In Iraq there are no mailboxes, no house numbers, and no street signs. The best we can do is use human intelligence to verify addresses, which leaves plenty of room for error. Still, this man could be an infiltrator and this could be the right house. That's where gut instinct comes in. I turn to Biggie.

"What do you think? Any chance he's lying?"

Biggie looks again at the clock face.

"No, he's Shi'a," he says. "No doubt."

I reach into my medical pouch, pull out my shears, and cut his hands free. He immediately rubs at his wrists. I take a last look at Abu Bakr's badge and credentials, then hand them back to him.

"*Shukran*," he says.

"I'm sorry about this," I say. "We are looking for an insurgent that lives in your neighborhood."

"Yes, I know," he replies, slipping his bifold back into the front of his dishdasha. "We are aware of his presence."

"I'm sorry?"

"We were watching him, but then he disappeared. He no longer lives here."

"So he's not one of the men in the courtyard?" I ask.

"No, all of them are Shi'a. The man we are looking for is Sunni that joined al Qaeda."

"What's his address?" I ask, concealing my cards.

"Eighty-two."

I look at Biggie. He raises his bushy eyebrows and shrugs his shoulders.

"I'm sorry about this," I say. "Obviously, we're at the wrong house."

"Okay," he says in English, then switches back to Arabic, which Biggie translates. "It is difficult to find these men, but it is important. They are ruining Iraq."

I nod in agreement. Then I put my hand out and he takes it in his. I put my second hand on his wrist.

"Thank you for helping to make Iraq safe," I say. "I'm sorry for all this trouble."

"No," he says, "it's okay. This helps my disguise. Now, no one will believe I'm the chief of police if the secret gets out."

I let go of his hand and leave him in his home. Outside in the courtyard I find the Alabama Lieutenant sipping from his CamelBak. His face is red as a beet. Mike joins us and I explain the situation to them.

"The chief of police?" the Lieutenant asks.

"Yes, the *undercover* chief of police," I reply.

"Damn," he says. "Well, if the man is not here, then let's load up."

"Roger that," I say.

The Lieutenant gives the order and the soldiers cut free the remaining men in the courtyard. I give instructions to Biggie and he makes a general announcement to the group, stating that we apologize for the mix-up. They nod with no signs of resentment, but I wonder if they can't help but be put off a little.

In two minutes we're loaded in the Strykers and I'm sticking out the rear porthole next to Mike. The formation pulls out and I watch the Iraqis walk back toward their homes. As we cruise down route FLORIDA toward the base, I catch a glimpse of the Kirkuk Citadel, the ancient Assyrian fortress that allegedly houses the remains of the prophet Daniel. The citadel looks like a medieval castle.

How many warriors have seen this citadel? For centuries, soldiers have been crossing these sands. Their uniforms, allegiances, and languages change, but their blood always bleeds the same color—red.

Templeton is still sitting behind a computer in the command post when I enter.

"Do you have a second?" I ask.

He looks up at me. "Sure."

"Can we talk outside?"

He gets up from his chair and follows me out the door. We stand face-to-face in the hot sun.

"I'm a little concerned about the impact we're having on civilians," I say.

"How so?" Templeton asks.

"We've raided several wrong houses lately, and we should be compensating these families."

"How do you want to compensate them?"

"Money."

"Sure, no problem," Templeton responds. "We have plenty of captured cash."

"And I need a few minutes before we leave to apologize to the head of each household, in front of the family."

"In front of the family?"

"It's an issue of pride for Iraqis. When we raid their houses, they feel disrespected. Taking a few minutes to restore that respect in front of their families will go a long way toward keeping them from becoming our future enemies."

Templeton nods in agreement and then offers up an argument. "You know, some of the guys say that this is the cost the Iraqis have to pay for freedom. That if they were to turn in the bad guys then they wouldn't have to endure our raids."

"I understand," I reply, "but you have to put yourself in their shoes. If they become snitches, they risk retaliation. If they don't, they risk our raids. They are between a rock and a hard place."

"Roger that," Templeton says, "but it's their country. We're just here to help them along until they get on their feet. And that means hunting down the foreign bastards that are ruining this place."

"Well, we're the ones who came here, not the other way around, but on the latter point we agree," I said. "So, do I get a couple of minutes?"

"Yeah, it makes sense. Just don't delay too long."

"Deal."

We shake hands to seal our agreement. Templeton has a tough job balancing the pressure to produce results versus the impact we are having on the locals. It's a challenge, especially in a country where our enemies wear no uniforms and don't play by the rules. It's an easy trap to descend to their level, to become like our enemy in trying to defeat him, but that's why we wear the uniform.

6

Power Lines

June 17, 2006

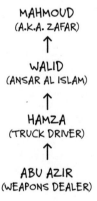

MAHMOUD
(A.K.A. ZAFAR)
↑
WALID
(ANSAR AL ISLAM)
↑
HAMZA
(TRUCK DRIVER)
↑
ABU AZIR
(WEAPONS DEALER)

I'm filled with pride watching the final seconds tick off the clock. It may prove to be one of the proudest moments of the U.S. Men's National Team, even though it wasn't a victory. In a tough match against one of the best teams in the history of the sport and the eventual World

Cup Champions, the United States draws with Italy 1–1. An Italian player was sent off halfway through the first half, forcing them to play down a man. Then two U.S. players were sent off with red cards in the last two minutes before halftime. The U.S. played the entire second half of the game with nine players to Italy's ten. It will prove to be the only game that Italy doesn't win in the 2006 World Cup.

"Helluva game," Mike says as we watch the teams shake hands and trade jerseys.

"A draw against Italy in the World Cup is an unbelievable result," I reply. "It feels like they've finally arrived on the world stage."

"I still prefer football," Mike says.

As we chuckle, the Bat Phone rings. Mike picks it up.

"Got it," he says and hangs up the phone.

He turns to me.

"Want to call it?" he asks.

"Let me guess. Meet at the Stryker in ten minutes?"

"Yes, but guess what else?" Mike asks.

"No idea," I reply.

"Mahmoud is home."

"Airguards!"

I stand up on the seat and open the hatch above me. I emerge into the cool night air rushing past my face. It feels a thousand degrees cooler than during our day mission. I lower the night-vision monocle and watch a green and black world pass by. We are racing down a narrow road in the midst of a middle class neighborhood. The Strykers barely fit between the stone houses on either side. I expect to scrape a wall at any second.

The homes are a mixture of one and two stories, old and new, clean and crumbling. I sweep the blur of rooftops, balconies, windows, and alleys. There's not a soul in sight. The lead vehicle stops at an intersection and the formation screeches to a halt behind it. Besides the low hum of the resting engines, it's silent. Nights are always like this in Kirkuk—after the sun goes down, people disappear. I've never seen an Iraqi at night except for inside our target homes. They disappear with the darkness.

The lead vehicle quickly turns and accelerates into the neighborhood and we follow. The houses encroach on the road and again there are mere inches on either side of the Stryker as we race down the street.

The lead vehicle turns again around a tight corner and our TC yells directions at our driver over the intercom. "Don't cut it too tight! Lead it! Lead it!"

We barely make it around a tight corner between two cinder-block walls that line the residential street. We move forward twenty yards and slam on the brakes. Soldiers pour out of the vehicles and the medic pulls on my leg. I lower myself from the porthole and jump off the ramp. As soon as my feet hit the ground there is an explosion. My night vision shuts down, drowned in bright light. Everyone freezes, waiting to hear the call for a medic, but it never comes. The light bursts again, followed by another thunderous crack.

The Stryker behind us missed the turn and had to back up. In doing so, the antennas on top of their vehicle clipped a set of power lines and became entangled. When the driver then pulled forward, he dragged the power lines with them, bending the wooden power pole and snapping it in half. At the same time that the pole snapped, a large electrical current overloaded a transistor and caused it to explode, sending a huge arc of electricity down the line. The result is a Fourth of July fireworks show. Sparks, cracks, and flashes continue to fill the night sky. The entire block goes black as the electric grid fails. The light show continues while the vehicle goes forward and backward attempting to free its antennae. After three attempts it finally breaks free and pulls up behind us. The fireworks show is over. Soldiers pile out of the Stryker and run past.

"Shall we?" I say to Mike.

"So much for the element of surprise," he replies.

We trot down the street with Biggie and Tiny in trail. Halfway down the block of two-story homes we find the soldiers set up on a house. As we approach, there's a small explosion, followed by the sound of metal falling onto stone. We wait by the wall for our call.

Two minutes later, the Alabama Lieutenant appears in the entranceway. "Okay, you guys are up."

"Mahmoud?" I ask.

"Not here," he says. "There's a woman and a small boy on the roof."

We walk through the gate and into the courtyard. Glass crunches beneath our boots as we cross the threshold. Inside, we climb three sets of stone stairways with no handrails. The floors that we pass are completely bare.

We exit onto the roof. It is dark except for the glow of green targeting beams. A woman and a small boy sit against a low wall while a soldier stands over them. I approach and kneel down in front of them, lifting the monocle from my eye. I turn on a small flashlight to view their faces. Mike and the terps kneel next to me.

"As-salamu alaykum," I say.

The woman is wearing a black head scarf and a patterned purple dress that covers her from wrist to ankle. Next to her a young boy in a white T-shirt and pants sits calmly staring. The woman answers me softly, avoiding eye contact.

"Alaykum as-salam."

"Everything is okay," I say through Biggie. "We're just going to ask you some questions and then we'll leave. No need to worry."

She doesn't respond.

"Who lives in this house?" I ask.

Biggie translates.

"Just my family," the woman responds.

"Who is in your family?"

"Just my husband, me, and my son."

"What is your husband's name?"

"Mahmoud."

"When did he leave?"

"This afternoon," she replies.

"What time this afternoon?"

"I don't know. It was after lunch."

"Was anyone with him?"

"No."

"How did he leave?"

"A friend came to pick him up in a car."

"Did he say where he was going?"

"No."

"Did he say when he was coming back?"

"He won't come back."

"Do you know where he might have gone?"

"No."

"Does he have relatives or friends in Kirkuk?"

"His relatives are not in Kirkuk. I never meet his friends."

"What is his job?"

"I don't know."

"Do you know the names of his friends?"

"No."

"How will you see him again?"

"I don't know."

I look around the roof. There is nothing. I turn to Mike and the terps. "Did you guys see any furniture on the way up?"

"The house is completely empty," Mike says.

"Yeah, there's nothing," Tiny adds.

I turn back to Mahmoud's wife. "How will you live here? There is nothing."

"I don't know."

"How will you eat?"

"I don't know," she says, and for the first time she appears to see my face. "He didn't leave us any money."

"Did he leave you any food?"

"No."

Biggie shakes his head as he relays the answer.

"What do you think?" I ask him.

"I don't know," he says. "Maybe she's telling the truth."

I turn to the woman. "What is your son's name?"

"Tamam."

"How old is Tamam?"

"He is seven."

I look at the young boy. He stares at my face with curiosity and inspects the pouches all over my body and the black rifle strapped to my vest.

"Can I ask your son some questions?"

"Yes," she replies.

I turn to the boy. "What is your name?"

Biggie gets closer to the boy and rubs his arm gently. He relays some words of comfort. The boy begins to talk.

"Tamam."

"What is your father's name?" I ask.

"Mahmoud."

"When did you see your father last?"

"After we ate."

"Did he say where he was going?"

"No."

"Did he say when he would be back?"

"No."

The whole time Biggie comforts the boy, complimenting him, rubbing his head. If you didn't know any better, you would think this was Biggie's own son. Tamam doesn't provide anything useful.

I look at Mike. "Do you have any questions?"

"Not really. I don't think we're going to get anywhere here."

"I agree," I say. "Do you have any of the Iraqi money on you?"

"Yes, I have a roll of bills in my pocket."

"Let's leave it with her."

"Good idea," Mike says and pulls a large wad of cash from his pocket.

I hand it to Biggie and he gives it to the woman and explains our gift. She quickly tucks it under her dress.

"Tell her I said that we're sorry to have scared her and that I hope they stay safe," I say to Biggie.

The big Iraqi translates my words and the woman nods.

"*Shukran,*" she says.

Thanks.

I take a last look at the face of the boy. He has Mahmoud's eyes.

* * *

On the way back to the base, we sit in silence and I contemplate our latest mission. I understand the criticism some might levy for giving money to a terrorist's wife. Maybe she supports him. Perhaps she hides things for him. The money we gave her may ultimately end up in Mahmoud's pocket and be used against Americans. Or maybe she knows nothing of his crimes. Those things really don't worry me because there are bigger dragons to slay.

Interrogations are a means to an end. This is counterinsurgency and the strategic objective is successfully choking off terrorist recruitment and protecting the population. Everything we do must help to achieve those ends.

When we go into a house and kill or capture a terrorist, we remove one guy from the insurgency. When we go into a house and detain an innocent guy, we may very well be creating dozens *more* terrorists. Raid missions invariably leave a lasting impression on the population. If we are going to win their hearts and minds, we have to conduct them the right way and can't take our eyes off the long-term goal.

One day, Tamam is going to grow up. He might not like U.S. policies in the Middle East, but that doesn't mean he will dislike Americans. The best way we can counter al Qaeda's ability to recruit is by, well, acting American. A little compassion can go a long way. It's like the old saying goes: You can attract more flies with honey than you can with vinegar.

Over fifty years ago, the United States was fighting communist insurgencies in Southeast Asia. Back then, we had all the same arguments we're having now about counterinsurgency. The dilemmas were spelled out in the fictional novel *The Ugly American* by Eugene Burdick and William Lederer, released in 1958. The book pointed toward the failure of strategies because government officials and diplomats lacked an understanding of local cultures. It is rumored that in 1959, Senator John F. Kennedy sent a copy of the book to every member of the U.S. Senate. We don't know if they read it. We subsequently failed at counterinsurgency in Vietnam.

Today's leading voices on counterinsurgency—David Kilcullen, General (retired) H. R. McMaster, Colonel (retired) John Nagl, General David Petraeus, and Andrew Exum, among others—offer a refreshing renewal of the counterinsurgency lessons from the 1950s with some insightful improvements. Most of this is not new. We are reinventing the wheel. Unfortunately for us, terrorists like Mahmoud, a.k.a. Zafar, don't afford time for lengthy debate. While we improve our methods, so does the enemy. Meanwhile, the cost is in lives.

7

Three Brothers

June 25, 2006

We've gone outside the wire every day for a week searching for new targets. When we don't have a target, we go trolling—that is, just looking. If we develop credible sources that provide information about insurgent activity, we launch. We need an avenue to Mahmoud. A few leads have developed from other forms of intelligence and we've chased those down to no avail—dry holes, wrong houses, or small fish. No one is leading up the ladder. The daily missions that take place any time, day or night, take their toll. You catch sleep when you can because you never know when the Bat Phone will ring next.

The exhaustion accumulates and builds to the point where it no longer matters. You're a zombie. You quit thinking about it. After we finish a mission, the raid team goes back to their quarters to play video games or rest, but our job is just beginning. After we inprocess the detainees, we interrogate them again to verify the information we received at the point-of-capture. It's another chance to get additional specifics about a target. It's not enough to know just the location, as plenty of homes have been booby-trapped. There are phone calls to analysts, meetings with the intelligence officer, and inspection of evidence collected at the scene—and, of course, reports to write. No interrogation is complete until the interrogation report has been sent off. The reports generate more questions for the detainees from analysts, which starts the whole cycle over again. This is the intelligence cycle in combat. Requirements, collections processing, analyzing, and publishing. Sometime during that process a mortar shakes your trailer or a roadside bomb misses your convoy. Combat life becomes a grind.

Often, Mike and I are greeted by the rising sun when we leave the interrogation booth and race to our trailers for a few hours' sleep before the next mission. Sometimes our heads never make it to our pillows. When they do, the enemy is nice enough to send us off to sleep awash in the sound of falling mortars. We ignore them.

After lunch, Mike and I return to the office. I watch an episode of *Band of Brothers* while Mike e-mails his wife.

Today, the cells next door are empty. The Bat Phone rings and Mike answers it. " 'Gators."

A voice on the other end.

"Got it. We'll head over and pick them up now."

Mike hangs up the phone.

"What's up?" I ask.

"The conventional guys rolled up some Iraqis that Jeff believes might know Mahmoud."

"That would be convenient," I say.

We jump in the SUV and head over to the other side of the base, past the big shiny BX—base exchange—and the chow hall. At the conventional forces prison we show our IDs and they invite us in.

We are greeted by a friendly Sergeant, a late-twenties interrogator with a buzz cut. Typically, there is friction between our task force and the conventional forces. They share information; we don't. Mike and I don't make the rules, but there are classification issues. If I were on the other side, I'd probably resent us. It's unusual for one of their interrogators to offer up detainees. No one likes to give up sources of information. When I was a young captain flying special-operations helicopters, my squadron commander used to say, "Every lion has a kingdom."

"You guys here for Moe, Larry, and Curly?" the Sergeant asks.

"We'll take them off your hands," Mike says.

"I think these guys are uninvolved but my commander,

after talking to your commander, thinks otherwise. There's something wrong with one of them," the Sergeant replies and hands us the detainees' screening reports. "He's a little off his rocker, if you don't mind my opinion."

There's a natural deference to anyone that works for the task force. The Sergeant doesn't know our rank or affiliation; all he knows is that his commander won't act on his hunch. It takes blind faith to assume that we will. I admire the Sergeant's instinct. He's what every interrogator should be—caring beyond his own world.

We sign the appropriate paperwork and a guard leads us back to a large cage. There are ten prisoners sitting on the ground in a fenced-in area. It looks like a zoo. Another guard joins the first and together they remove our three prisoners, place them in flexi-cuffs, and pass them to us. One of them, the youngest, is hunched over and stays that way as we walk outside. We lead them to the SUV and drive across the base to our compound where we unload them into our cell block. The young hunched-over guy mumbles and rocks in his seat the whole way.

"What's up with that guy?" Mike asks.

"No idea," I say.

Two of the men are in their forties, medium build, one with a brown beard and the other with a black mustache. We review their screening reports and learn that the three men are brothers, captured in their home; the only information Jeff has is that they may be family relations of

Mahmoud. Sometimes intelligence works that way. You get a guy with very little info and you have to start from scratch. Sometimes you start with nothing.

The Doc comes over to the compound and evaluates the three men, documenting the fact that they have no injuries. The hunched-over guy doesn't respond to questioning. He just sits in his chair, rocking back and forth and mumbling under his breath. He won't follow the Doc's basic commands. The Doc calls me in with Biggie. I find the Doc standing in front of the guy with a tongue depressor in his hand.

"I can't even look in this guy's mouth," he says.

Biggie tries talking to him but the guy pays no attention. Biggie waves a hand in front of his face but the young man takes no notice. I look at the screening report.

"His name is Rafiq," I say.

Biggie tries calling his name, rubbing his shoulder lightly, and shaking his hand.

Nothing. Rafiq just rocks in the chair, mumbling. Mike and Tiny walk into the adjacent room and we join them.

"What do you think, Doc?" I ask.

"He's mentally challenged," the Doc replies. "I tried several things—light in his eyes, snapping next to his ears from behind when he couldn't see me . . . nothing."

"He could be faking," I say. "We should question his brothers."

"Let's ask them if he's mentally handicapped," Mike says.

"Or . . ." I say, "let's tell them that he started acting normal and admitted that he was faking."

"Good idea," Tiny chimes in.

"And ask them what age this started and what are his symptoms," Mike adds. "Then we can compare stories."

"Perfect," I say.

Biggie and I take the brother with the beard, and Mike and Tiny take the one with the mustache. We settle down in an interrogation room and I remove the man's flexi-cuffs with my shears. He rubs at his wrists.

"As-salamu alaykum," I say.

"Alaykum as-salam."

He has a long, straight face and wears no expression. Biggie translates.

"Dani, right?" I ask.

"Yes, that is my name."

"It's a pleasure to meet you, Dani."

"You too," he says.

"I want to ask you some questions about your brother, Rafiq."

A frown comes over his face.

"He stopped moving around and mumbling," I say. "He admitted he was faking."

"That's not possible!" Dani says. "He is not faking!"

"How long has he been like this?" I ask.

"Five years."

"Why?"

"He was in a car accident and injured his brain."

"How does he eat?" I ask.

"My mother feeds him," Dani replies.

"Does he talk?"

"Sometimes he will yell if he is angry."

"What did the doctors tell you?"

"They said that he has a permanent injury to his brain."

I ask several more questions and then, satisfied, I meet Mike in the hallway.

"What does your guy say?" I ask.

"He says Rafiq was in a car accident five years ago and has a brain injury. He said he's always like this, but sometimes he gets really angry. What about your guy?"

"Same."

We compare more details and they match.

"I guess the guy is not faking," I say.

"Well, that's what the Doc said," Mike replies.

I go to the guards and make sure that they know Rafiq is mentally disabled. I instruct them to give him a cot to sleep on versus the plywood floor. The whole time he rocks and mumbles.

We return to the two brothers. Biggie and I sit down again in front of Dani.

"I'm making sure your brother is taken care of," I say.

"*Shukran*," he replies.

"Who lives in your house?" I ask.

"Just my brothers, our wives, and our mother."

I run through the names of his family members, including all of his cousins in Kirkuk. There's no Mahmoud. I ask him about his neighbors, co-workers, and in-laws. Still no Mahmoud. I continue for three hours and, on breaks, Mike and I compare notes. The brothers' stories match exactly. After another hour of questioning, we visit Jeff in the command post. He's sitting behind his computer, typing.

"What's up, guys?" he says.

"We have nothing from those three guys we took from the other side of the base," I say.

"Yeah, it was a pretty weak link," he admits.

"One of them is mentally disabled," Mike says.

"Well, they can take care of him at the main facility."

"Huh?" I say. "You mean we're not going to release them?"

"No, someone thinks the young guy is a foreign fighter."

"Why would they think that?" Mike asks.

"Not sure," Jeff says. "But they are going to the main facility today."

Mike and I shrug our shoulders and shake our heads.

"Let them figure out the same," I say. "Then they can release them from down there."

"It's a long taxi ride back," Mike says.

I've been through this routine before. At the main

prison we rescued a kidnap victim who'd been tortured and held for ransom by an al Qaeda cell of thugs. I couldn't get him a thirty-minute ride to his employer's office. The powers that be kicked him out the front gate. I gave him a hundred dollars of my own money to bribe his way to safety, if need be.

We cross the compound to return to our office. Along the way, we spot the guards loading the three brothers into the back of an SUV, the youngest brother hunched over and rocking.

As soon as we step foot back in our office and sit down, the Bat Phone rings.

" 'Gators," Mike answers. "Roger."

He hangs up.

"No need to say it," I say. "I can tell by the look on your face."

The sun is setting as I lift myself out the porthole. There's no need for night-vision in the fading light. We cruise down route FLORIDA, the only other vehicles in sight a semitrailer convoy with Humvee escorts that we pass going in the other direction—the BX's weekly delivery of Power Bars, energy drinks, video games, and *Maxim*.

We turn off the main highway and onto a two-lane

road. The sun dips below the horizon; there is not an Iraqi in sight. We cruise past the ancient Kirkuk Citadel, its brick walls colored shades of orange in the fading light.

We enter a residential neighborhood, make a few turns, and wedge between two high walls guarding middle-class homes. We slow to a crawl, and then stop. I scan the rooftops and windows with an infrared beam.

"Nice neighborhood," I whisper to Mike over the low rumble of the Stryker's engine.

"This is no shantytown," Mike replies.

In the distance a dog barks.

"I think we're trolling," I say.

"Definitely," Mike replies.

A shadow passes quickly in front of a window on the second story of the home in front of me. I aim my beam through the window and into a room, placing a red dot on the wall. The shadow doesn't return.

The formation starts up again. We cruise through the neighborhood and rejoin the two-lane road, then accelerate on the highway. Mike and I take our places back inside the Stryker, only to be called again to the airguard position fifteen minutes later. It's dark and I switch to my night-vision monocle and laser.

We enter another neighborhood of middle-class homes. Again, the homes are protected on either side of the wide street by stone walls. It's quiet and deserted. We slow to a stop and I scan the rooftops and windows, but this time my beam is green, invisible to the naked eye.

The rear hatches drop and soldiers race toward the home directly adjacent to our Stryker. They quickly line up next to the gate and the medic pulls on my pant leg. I descend into the hold, sit, and wait. Mike sits across from me doing the same. A small explosion is followed by the sound of metal falling onto stone.

Two minutes later, Mike and I and the terps exit the Stryker and trot to the house. Inside are two middle-aged brothers, their round bellies draped by white dishdashas, standing in the kitchen with their hands tied behind their backs. The Alabama Lieutenant comes down the stairs and joins us.

"We have these two here," he says, "and the boys are hitting the house next door. One of you come with me."

I look at Mike.

"I'll go," I say.

"I'll get started here," Mike says.

The Lieutenant looks at me.

"Follow me," he says.

Biggie and I follow the Lieutenant out the door, down the street, and into the next house. On our way in, we pass soldiers running in the opposite direction toward the gate.

"Squirters," one of them says as he passes. "They ran out the back as we entered."

In the courtyard is an Iraqi man sitting Indian-style with his hands flexi-cuffed behind his back. He has thick black framed glasses and a bushy black mustache. The Lieutenant heads toward the gate.

"I'll be back," he says.

I approach the captured Iraqi; before I can speak he questions me in English.

"What have I done?" he asks with a scowl.

I kneel down in front of him with Biggie.

"You can speak English?" I ask.

"Of course," he responds.

"What is your name?"

"Abu Akil," he replies.

"What is your job?"

"I am a university professor."

"What do you teach?"

"English and literature."

"Who lives in this house?" I ask.

I am barking up a tree that I know nothing about. I'm not sure why we hit the first house, but our trolling expedition is now an official block party.

"I live here with my wife and my son."

"Do you know why we are here?"

"I have no idea," he says.

"I think you know," I bluff.

I have nothing, so a little gamble will do me no harm.

"I know," he replies.

"Why?" I ask.

He rolls his shoulders to relieve the discomfort. I pull out my shears and cut his hands free. He rubs at his wrists.

"So tell me, why do you think we are here?" I ask again.

He lowers his voice to a whisper.

"Because of my neighbor," he replies.

"What about your neighbor?" I ask.

"You already know."

"Yes, but I need you to confirm it."

"No thank you," he says. "I have a family."

"No one needs to know it came from you," I reply. "Besides, I already know."

"I would like to help, but you have to understand. No one is safe."

"Just to be sure," I say, "which neighbor are you talking about?"

"The one across the street."

"Wait here," I instruct Biggie.

I stand and head out the gate. In the street I find the Lieutenant.

"What's up?" he asks.

"My guy says that he thought we were coming for the man across the street, but he won't say why."

"Really?"

"Yes, but there's no way to tell if he's trying to settle an old score."

I haven't encountered it, but others report running into this trap.

"Well, there's only one way to find out," the Lieutenant says.

He speaks into his mic and in seconds there is a team of soldiers lined up next to him.

"We'll call you when we are ready," he says and disappears with the team out the gate.

I return to the courtyard and kneel down in front of the professor.

"Why do you think we came for your neighbor?" I ask.

"Many people visit his house," he says. "There are rumors."

A small explosion fills the air, followed by the sound of metal falling onto stone.

"What type of rumors?" I ask.

"He was a general in the military under Saddam."

This peaks my interest. The men who ran the early insurgent networks were former Saddam-era flag officers—Baathists. Many of the guys on the infamous Deck of Cards were former generals. Might we have gotten lucky?

A soldier appears in the entrance to the courtyard.

"You're needed across the street," he says.

"Can you watch this guy?" I ask.

"Sure," he says.

"I removed his flexi-cuffs," I say as I make my way into the street.

Biggie follows.

Glass crunches beneath my boots as I cross through the entrance of the house and into the living room. Our newest capture is a man in his sixties with a bald head and gray hair around his ears. He has a matching gray mustache and wears a white dishdasha. His hands are flexi-cuffed and a soldier stands watch nearby. As I approach, he smiles.

"Hello," he says in English.

"Hello," I say.

"What is your name?"

"Shafi."

"Nice to meet you, *General* Shafi," I reply.

"The pleasure is mine," he replies. "How can I help you?"

Is he running an approach on me? I'm suspicious of his casual friendliness so I decide to twist it.

"I think you know already, since you have been expecting us," I say.

"Yes, but I think it's better if we talk back at your base."

"You want to go back to the base?" I ask.

"It's safer," he replies.

"Fine with me," I say.

I find the Lieutenant in the courtyard talking to Mike. I explain the situation to them.

"Well, then, let's load him up," the Lieutenant says.

"Anything from your guys?" I ask Mike.

"Nothing," he says.

This is a cluster. Our original target and the house next to it turn up nothing. But a random Iraqi rats out his neighbor. There's a lot to be suspicious of, but maybe we just got very lucky.

The Lieutenant barks orders. I return to the house and gather General Shafi and together, with Biggie, escort him to our Stryker.

General Shafi sits on the edge of a cot in a special room we have for detainees that we want to make comfortable. We call it the Soft Room. Mike sits beside me.

"General Shafi, it is an honor to meet you," I start.

"Thank you for bringing me here," he says.

"So you know why we came?" I ask.

"Yes, I do."

The truth is that I know nothing other than the tidbit of information I received from his neighbor. Jeff ran his biographical data through a database and it came up empty.

"Why don't you start at the beginning?" I say.

"Do you mean when I was in the air force?" he asks.

I thought he was army.

"Yes," Mike says, "what was your last unit?"

"I commanded the fighter squadron at Al Asad Airbase."

"What type of fighters?" I ask.

"MIGs and Frogfoots."

I saw satellite photos while in Saudi Arabia before the ground war started. The Iraqis buried many of their aircraft in the desert in an ill-fated attempt to save them.

"Did you fly?" I ask.

"I was a pilot a long time ago," General Shafi replies.

Since I flew for six years, we make small talk about flying. We move our hands through the air and have a few good laughs sharing near-death experiences. It's a jovial atmosphere, until I break it.

"General Shafi," I say finally, "excuse me for being blunt, but let's talk about why we came to your house."

"Okay," he says. "I'm open to your questions."

"Why don't you start off by telling me about your involvement?" I say carefully.

"Well," he says, "my involvement started just after the end of ground operations. That was when I first contacted the Americans who came to Al Asad."

"What did you talk about?" I ask.

"I told them where we buried the planes," he says.

"Right," Mike says, "but we want to talk about your involvement in the current situation."

"Oh, okay," the general replies. "Well, I've been tracking people as you know, since we last spoke."

"When did we last speak?" I ask.

"Six months ago," he says.

"Who exactly did you speak to?" I ask.

"I think his name was Mister Chris," General Shafi replies. "He never told me who he worked for."

"Do you have his contact information?" I ask.

"Yes, it is back at the house," he replies. "Don't you work with Mister Chris?"

"People come and go often," Mike says, covering quickly.

"Yes, this is one of your problems," General Shafi replies. "Every six months I see a new face."

"What were you helping Chris with?" I ask.

"He gave me a list of former generals that he wanted me to find," he says. "I have found a couple of them, even though it is very dangerous for me."

I turn to Mike; he wears the same stone face, masking surprise. Our accidental capture is a source for our own government? What unit or agency does Chris work for? The lines between other governmental agencies and military organizations often cross, but this is unreal.

"How is it dangerous?" Mike asks.

"If the terrorists find out, they will kill me and my family," General Shafi explains. "No one in my neighborhood knows who I am."

I hesitate to inform him that his neighbor knows something is up, then decide that it's best not to reveal my entire hand. What if the general is lying in an attempt to find out what we know?

"Where are these two other generals?" I ask.

"In the ground," he answers.

"You mean underground?" Mike asks.

"No, they are dead."

"And the others?" I ask.

"I'm still working on it."

We gather the information that General Shafi has collected and committed to memory, then pay a visit to Jeff in the command post.

"He claims to be a source of Mister Chris," Mike says.

"I can look him up in the source database," Jeff says. "Previously I only looked in the terrorist database."

He turns to his computer and starts clicking. Seconds later he looks up from his screen.

"Yup, here he is. Shafi Khudair. General. Iraqi Air Forces."

"So we captured one of our own sources?" I ask.

"Looks like it," Jeff says. "It says he was assigned to 'Other Governmental Agency.' "

"Does Other Governmental Agency have a name?" Mike asks.

"Nope," Jeff replies, "it doesn't say."

Templeton enters the command post and walks over.

"What's up, guys?" he asks.

"Our captured general is one of OGA's informants," Jeff replies. "He's in the database."

Templeton shakes his head.

"Does he know anything?" he asks.

"He knows the location of two former Saddam-era generals," I reply.

"Really? Where?"

"In the ground," Mike says.

Anyone who's worked in government intelligence has hit this hurdle at some point in their career—another agency has information and doesn't share it. Our task force doesn't share info with the conventional guys. The OGA doesn't share information with us. Someone, somewhere doesn't share information with OGA for fear that they will take over their source. I know the game all too well. Every lion has his kingdom.

After 9/11, tremendous emphasis was put on intelligence sharing, but there are limits. Many of those limits exist because of archaic thinking in terms of turf. Giving up information could mean giving up targets, which could mean giving up missions, which could mean giving up resources. We'd be better off if we created a National Intelligence Service. Everyone who works in U.S. intelligence would be assigned to the NIS operationally and under the control of one commander, but would remain administratively controlled by their parent organization. It's the same concept for how the military organizes and fights wars with four separate services (the combatant command structure). It's that age-old principle of unity of command. It doesn't exist in intelligence and we all pay for it.

Meanwhile, as we're rolling up OGA sources, Mahmoud is still out there. And he's due to strike again while we're spinning our wheels.

8

Hamza

Once an Army is involved in war, there is a beast in every fighting man which begins tugging at its chains . . . a good officer must learn early on how to keep the beast under control both in his men and in himself.

—GENERAL GEORGE C. MARSHALL

July 1, 2006

Cristiano Ronaldo, the Portuguese star of Manchester United, lines up behind the ball placed on the penalty hash mark. On the sideline are some of his club teammates, members of the English National Team, but on this day Ronaldo represents his homeland—Portugal. He is the fifth and final Portuguese player to make an attempt in this penalty shoot-out. If he makes it, game over. Portugal will advance to the semifinals for the first time in forty years. His Portuguese teammates stand in a row, arms thrown over shoulders, in anguished anticipation. Ronaldo starts his run toward the ball. A Portuguese population of over ten million watches along with two American interrogators sitting in eight-hundred-dollar ergonomic chairs next to a Bat Phone in northern Iraq. Ronaldo strikes the ball and it sails toward the right side of the net. The English goalkeeper dives left. The ball coasts into the back of the goal and the crowd erupts.

"That's a finish," I say.

"Almost makes me want to keep watching soccer," Mike replies.

It's been almost three weeks since we snatched the list from Abu Azir and we have yet to catch another member of his cell. Word must have spread quickly after his capture because each time our unit attempts to confirm the location of another member on the list, we discover an empty house. As usual, when there are no targets we go trolling. Not a day goes by that we don't carry out a mission. More than half of our raids are wrong houses. Our only successful raid since Abu Azir was the visit to Mahmoud's house and the interview of his wife, yet even that provided little valuable information. Still, our spooks continue to monitor the houses on the list for activity.

The Bat Phone rings.

" 'Gators," Mike answers. "Yeah. Okay. No problem."

He hangs up the phone.

"Stryker in ten minutes?" I ask.

"For once . . . no," he replies. "It was the spook. He needs Biggie for a mission."

"What's up with their terps?" I ask.

As a member of my team, I feel obligated to look out

for Biggie, without whom I cannot do my job. Biggie and I go way back to my arrival in Iraq. He was one of the first terps I worked with at our main prison. I'll never forget an interrogation that we worked together in which I interviewed a former fedayee (one of Saddam's elite bodyguards) turned al Qaeda operational commander. I ran a very intense emotional approach on the guy, hoping to draw a human response out of a rock-hard disposition, and in doing so I used a technique called "the Van Gogh"—so named because I paint in the mind of the detainee a picture of the future of Iraq.

I had described, through Biggie's translation, a scene in which Iraq has become a Middle Eastern Disneyland and American and Iraqi kids walk down the street hand in hand without fear for their safety. As the former fedayee struggled to hold back tears, Biggie stood up and ran out of the room. Tears pouring down his face, he wailed in anguish. He proceeded to pound on the wall outside the interrogation room in despair. The scene I had painted completely overwhelmed his composure—I'd broken my terp.

The next day, with a lot of hard work by another member of my interrogation team, the fedayee collapsed and became one of our best sources of information, allowing us to wipe from the earth several al Qaeda cells outside Baghdad. After that experience, I knew that inside Biggie's large frame was a gentle giant.

"All of their terps are out on other missions," Mike replies. "He says it's urgent."

"I'll tell Biggie," I say.

I walk next door to the terps' office. I say office, but it's more like a den—a cubbyhole of plywood walls attached to a large building where we store confiscated evidence. Inside the den is a small color television and a few folding chairs. Against one wall are two bunk beds built of leftover two-by-fours and plywood. When the terps aren't in their den watching television or outside smoking, they are in the morale room across the compound using the phones to call their wives back in the States.

A good terp is like gold. Not only is the terp a skilled translator, he or she is a cultural encyclopedia. In the chase for Zarqawi, several times it was terps who made crucial inputs to interrogation techniques or in our analysis of detainees. Most of these men and women grew up in Iraq and know the culture. They introduce some biases because they are Shi'a (we have no Sunni Iraqi terps). One of our terps had three brothers assassinated when al Qaeda discovered he was working for Americans. He continued to work for us, although the emotional toll on him eventually caused his performance to deteriorate to the point that we had to send him back to the States to recover, and grieve. Most Americans cannot appreciate the sacrifices that Muslim-Americans have made in this

war and in Afghanistan. There are Muslim-American soldiers buried at Arlington National Cemetery.

I received a chain e-mail while I was in Iraq. You may
have seen it. The e-mail asserts that all Muslims are terrorists and that violence is inevitable under Islam. I replied to
every name on the distribution list. My message was simple: I invited every one of them to come to Iraq and take
Biggie's place and sit next to me in the Stryker every day as
we departed the safety of our base and braved roadside
bombs, mortars, snipers, and suicide bombers. I asked
them if they would be willing to replace this Muslim-
American who risked his life for his adopted country. I'm
not so naïve as to neglect his vested self-interest in helping
American policies that benefit Shi'a Iraqis, but many terps
have died or been wounded in the line of duty. They are
contributing to our mission and serving America. Not sur-
prisingly, no one on the distribution list took up my offer.

Biggie and Tiny are sitting on the folding chairs drinking tea and watching music videos when I enter their den.
An attractive Middle Eastern woman in modern Western
clothes sings and dances on the television.

"Watching another al Qaeda recruiting video?" I ask.

"No," Tiny says, "this girl is Lebanese."

"Time to load up?" Biggie asks.

"Yes and no," I answer. "The spooks need you for a
mission."

Biggie nods in acknowledgement.

"What about their terps?" Tiny asks.

"They are out on other missions," I say. "Sorry, Biggie, but they say it's important."

"Okay," he says.

No complaints. The big Iraqi stands, lifts his body armor from the bottom bunk, and straps it on over his T-shirt while I enjoy the Lebanese singer. Biggie puts on a second shirt over the body amor, says something to Tiny in Arabic, good-bye to me, and heads for the door.

"Be careful," I say. "We'll see you when you get back."

He walks across the compound through the slush of pebbles to the spooks' office. I think of the hate e-mail and it turns my stomach.

The spooks drive a beat-up, dark blue Japanese SUV. They have bushy beards and wear white dishdashas to pass for Iraqis. In back, Biggie sits next to their source—an Iraqi. They don't talk. The spook steers the SUV toward the center of town on a two-lane road. Just before the city center, they come upon a police roadblock and slow down. Two Iraqi policemen in khaki uniforms with AK-47s guard the road. The spook pulls up, stops, and rolls down the window. The policeman approaches cautiously from the driver's side and spots Biggie and the source in the back through the open window. Biggie is sweating profusely in the midday heat. His shirt is stained with sweat and his body armor bulges over his big frame.

Just as the spook behind the wheel attempts an Arabic greeting, the policeman on his side of the vehicle quickly raises his AK-47 and aims at Biggie.

"A vest!" he shouts in Arabic. "He's wearing a suicide vest!"

The other policeman raises his rifle and points it at Biggie through the passenger compartment. The source throws his hands in the air.

"Your hands! Show me your hands!" the first policeman yells.

Biggie instantly raises his hands in the air. The spooks in the front yell, "We're Americans! We're Americans!"

"He's got a bomb!" the first policeman continues to yell. "Underneath his shirt!"

"It's my protective vest!" Biggie yells.

"We're Americans! Americans!" the spooks yell louder.

"I'm with them!" Biggie says.

The first policeman takes a step back, holding his rifle steady, finger on the trigger.

"Lift your shirt!" he orders. "Slowly!"

Biggie slowly reaches down, his hands shaking violently, and lifts his shirt. The policeman sees his body armor and drops his weapon.

"Goddamit!" one of the spooks yells.

Biggie drops his shirt. Sweat pours down his forehead.

"I'm sorry," the policeman says. "I thought it was a bomb vest."

"We're Americans," the spook behind the wheel says. "He works with us."

"Okay, okay," the second policeman says. "You can go. No problem, no problem."

The spooks shake their heads in disbelief. One of them turns around.

"You okay?" he asks Biggie.

Biggie opens his mouth, but no words come out.

"They almost shot him!" Tiny says.

We're standing outside the terp den and Biggie is inside lying down on the bottom bunk.

"That was close," Mike says.

"Is he okay?" I ask.

"He's okay," Tiny says. "He just wants to rest. He wants me to ask you if he can take the night off?"

I have no other terps. Usually we have five terps but we're down to two—one went home on leave, another was permanently borrowed by the spooks, and one was sent back to the main prison to help out with their numerous post-Zarqawi captures. If the Bat Phone rings and we go out on a mission, I have to take both Biggie and Tiny. It would slow us down too much for us to share a terp.

"I wish I could," I say, "but there's only you and Biggie. If the phone rings . . ."

"No problem," Tiny says. "He'll do it. He's just shook up."

I enter the den. Biggie is lying on his back with his eyes shut. His hand is pinching his nose between his eyes.

"I heard what happened," I say. "Are you okay?"

He doesn't move. "I'm okay, but I don't want to go with them again."

"Don't worry," I reply. "Next time I'll send Tiny."

"I should look at the bright side," Biggie says. "If he had shot me, at least I would have been wearing body armor."

Jeff sits behind his desk in the command post shuffling through papers. There are rows upon rows of addresses, phone numbers, and names—analyst work—connecting the dots. There is no functional central database for all this information, so analysts are often left to sort through it all manually.

"What's up?" I say.

He adjusts his glasses on his nose. "Not much. Just comparing the names and addresses from Abu Azir's list to other known insurgents."

"Any luck?"

"Nothing."

Jeff reaches across his desk and hands me a report. It's an Iraqi newspaper article translated into English. If only I'd refused to read it.

A few months ago an Iraqi female television reporter was kidnapped, along with her cameraman, while covering the Golden Dome Mosque bombing in Samarra, which happened in February. Iraqi police recently recovered a videotape that the kidnappers forced the cameraman to record. On it, the female reporter is strapped to a chair and a dozen holes are drilled in her arms and legs with a power tool. After that, they decapitate her. Then, they put the cameraman in front of his own camera and do the same to him. Hollywood couldn't make this stuff up.

I place the report on Jeff's desk and he drops the lists in his hands.

"Pretty gruesome, huh?" he says.

"Absolutely horrible," I say.

"That's what we're up against here."

"Sometimes, it's all so surrealistic," I reply. "Like a George Orwell novel gone really bad."

"Sort of puts into perspective why it's so important to catch these guys," Jeff says. "So we can stop this insanity."

"Definitely," I say.

It's not the first time the urge for revenge has boiled up inside me. I felt this before, when we watched al Qaeda propaganda videos back at the main prison. I watched as terrorists unloaded a bus of Shi'a passengers and then went down the line shooting each one in the head. I saw a man cut another man's head off with a machete. Yet this written report, which doesn't include images, is worse. There's something about the sheer brutality of it, about it being violence just for the sake of violence, that disturbs me.

Back at the main prison, I interrogated many hardcore al Qaeda members. Despite the horrible acts they had committed I still viewed them as human beings, was still able to find a way to work with them. I had to reach way down inside to find what remained of their emotional being, their "human-ness," and I was always able to generate some small amount of compassion for them regardless of what they had done.

When you read a report like this one, however, it draws out a beast deep inside you. It enrages you, yet suddenly it becomes very clear how the cycle of violence perpetuates itself and becomes a rapidly increasing downward spiral. You understand how it spins out of control. You can feel the chaos setting in. The beast starts tugging at its chains. It becomes difficult to separate your emotions from your duty—but that is exactly what our obligations as soldiers require.

I recall why I volunteered to come to Iraq—to make a difference, to make things better. I reject the cycle of violence and hold true to my principles. This is what it means to be a professional soldier. This is why we wear the uniform.

Jeff looks at my red face.

"Hard to get the images out of your head?" he asks.

"Yes," I reply. "Very difficult."

Jeff pushes his glasses back up his nose. "Maybe we'll get lucky and catch Zafar or Mahmoud, or whatever he calls himself, and put an end to this."

"They are getting desperate," I say. "The violence is getting worse."

"They are backed into a corner. Did you hear about the snipers?"

"Snipers?"

"The conventional guys across the base have lost three men to snipers in the last month. The last one was this week—a lieutenant was shot in the neck while pulling airguard."

I consider the next ring of the Bat Phone.

"The best we can do, then, is to finish this," I reply.

Jeff picks up the lists and starts comparing them again.

"Yup," he says, "it's time to finish it."

I turn for the door. Before I take two steps Jeff yells, "Holy shit!"

I turn around. "What's up?"

"A match! These addresses match!"

"Who? Which addresses?"

Jeff follows a line on the paper with his finger to a name. "Hamza."

"Hamza?"

"Yes, I remember this guy now. His name came up before. The truck driver suspected of transporting weapons to and from Iran."

"There's a lot of information about cooperation between al Qaeda and Iran. Ironic, no? Considering that al Qaeda is targeting Shi'a civilians here in Iraq and Iran is Shi'a?"

"This war has produced all sorts of strange bedmates," Jeff replies.

"So when do we go after this guy?" I ask.

"You should go put on your gear," Jeff advises. "Templeton will want us out the gate immediately."

Our convoy of Strykers rolls down route FLORIDA in the blazing heat. The back of the vehicle is a sauna and we sit in silence, exchanging grins that acknowledge the worthlessness of the fan. The TC yells directions to the driver from outside his porthole.

"Slow! Slow! Okay, cut it hard!"

On the black-and-white monitor at the front, I watch the scene go from a highway in the desert to a middle-class neighborhood of multilevel homes. We turn onto something very rare: a wide street.

"Airguards!"

Mike and I raise ourselves through the hatches. I raise my weapon and scan for targets. The streets are littered with garbage. The convoy slows to a crawl. On my side of the Stryker in the grass median I see an object that is completely out of place: a garbage can.

I attended tactical training before our deployment at the Federal Law Enforcement Training Center in Glynco, Georgia. On the way to work every morning from our hotel, our instructors challenged us to simulate driving in Iraq so that we would develop good habits. We practiced force protection (antiterrorism) measures such as always leaving space between our vehicle and the one in front at a stop so that we would have room to get away, if need be. One morning they placed a large cardboard box with Arabic writing on it on a street corner where we had to turn to get to work. About 10 percent of the class picked up on it. I wasn't one of them. The lesson: Always be on the lookout for objects that are out of place, especially in the absence of people.

There's not a soul in sight as the convoy continues to slow and the garbage can nears. The convoy halts and our driver stops our vehicle with the garbage can directly in front of me. There's absolutely no way to make oneself small while sticking outside a porthole scanning for targets. You suck it up. I stare at the garbage can. If only Oscar the Grouch would emerge.

After what feels like an eternity, the formation starts up again. We accelerate to fifty miles an hour and the houses fly by. The convoy makes a quick deceleration, turns, and then races a hundred meters down a residential street and screeches to a stop. The soldiers pour out of the vehicles and the medic pulls on my pant leg.

Inside the house, the soldiers capture an old man in a white dishdasha with a head of white hair and a white beard. The soldiers place him in the kitchen with his hands flexi-cuffed behind his back. He groans loudly. In a utility room off the kitchen another soldier stands over a woman in a black burkha with three children.

"I'll take the mother and kids this time," I say to Mike.

"Roger that," he replies.

The mother is sitting with the kids on the floor against a wall. The oldest of the children is a teenage girl and next to her is a preteen boy. The youngest of the children sits in her mother's lap—a toddler.

I kneel down in front of the mother and Biggie kneels beside me. On the intelligence sheet in my top pocket is the name of our target—Hamza.

"*As-salamu alaykum,*" I say.

"*Alaykum as-salam,*" the woman replies.

"What is your name?" I ask.

Biggie begins to translate. "Maya."

"Maya, who lives in this house?"

"My husband, my husband's brother, and my children."

"Who is the man in the kitchen?"

"That is my husband's brother, Abbas."

"What is your husband's name?"

"Abu Hamza."

Father of Hamza. Bingo.

"How many children do you have?" I ask.

"Four," she replies.

"There are three here, who is the fourth?"

"My oldest, Hamza."

My first reaction is to ask when he was at the house last, but then it hits me. The mother will lie to protect her son. I turn to the eldest girl. Biggie, sensing where I'm going with this, pats the hand of the child.

"Hello," I say with a smile.

The girl smiles shyly.

"Can you tell me when Hamza was last here?"

"He left this morning," she says.

I turn to her younger brother. "Is this true?"

"Yes," he says. "He drives a truck."

I turn back to the mother. "Your son drives a truck?"

"Yes, he delivers goods to Iran," she says.

"Do you know when he'll be back?"

"No. He's usually gone for a couple of weeks."

I turn to the children. "Did Hamza tell you when he would be back?"

They shake their heads negatively.

"*Shukran*," I say to the mother and give Biggie a nod toward the kitchen.

Mike is still questioning the uncle through Tiny. The Iraqi's hands are no longer bound and he speaks with them freely. He is visibly upset, his face filled with concern.

"He's saying, 'Why? Why? Why?'" Tiny says. "He just keeps repeating it. I think something is wrong with him."

Tiny puts a hand on the old man's shoulder to comfort him.

"It's okay," Tiny says. "Don't worry. Everything will be alright."

The man keeps repeating the same word—*why*. I pull Mike and Biggie aside.

"The mother says her son's name is Hamza and the kids say that he left this morning in his truck for Iran. They don't know when he'll be back."

"This guy doesn't know anything," Mike says. "I can't even get his name. Do we take him back?"

Everyone looks at me to make the call. I don't want to bring the old man back to the base, but he might have more information about Hamza's whereabouts, acquaintances, and when he'll return.

"We take him," I say, "but no flexi-cuffs. And make sure he's comfortable."

Mike nods in agreement. The Alabama Lieutenant appears from outside and strolls up.

"Get anything?" he asks.

"This is the right house. There's a Hamza that lives here that left this morning in his truck for Iran."

"I'll be damned!" the Lieutenant says.

"The old man in the kitchen is his uncle, but he's a little crazy. We're going to take him back to the base and ask him some more questions."

"That's fine," the Lieutenant says. "Anything else?"

"No one claims to know when he'll be back. The mother says he's usually gone for a couple of weeks."

The Lieutenant wipes at his sweaty forehead. "Okay then, let's load up and head back."

I return with Biggie to the mother in the utility room.

"I'm going to take your husband's brother back to base so that I can ask him a few more questions," I say.

"No, no!" she replies. "He is just an old man! He doesn't know anything!"

"I'll take care of him. Don't worry. I'll bring him back tomorrow."

"He's just an old man!" she insists.

"Here is some money," I say, and hand her a roll of Iraqi cash from our confiscated funds.

She takes it from my hand and tucks it under her dress.

"He's just an old man," she repeats, albeit more softly.

"I promise I'll take care of him," I say.

Biggie and I turn to leave. The young boy says something emphatically to his mother.

"What did he say?" I ask Biggie as we head for the door.

"He doesn't want us to take his uncle."

Abbas sits uneasily in the plastic chair in the interrogation room. Biggie and Mike sit at my side. The room is a cramped, plywood sauna. There's no air-conditioning. I hand Abbas a cold one-liter bottle of water.

"I just want to ask you a few questions," I begin.

"Why? Why?" the old man starts up again.

He repeated this the whole time on our journey from his house to the base. At times he raises his hands next to his head for emphasis.

"I just want to know if you spoke with Hamza this morning," I continue.

"Why? Why?" the old man says.

"Hamza," I say a little louder.

"Why? Why?"

"Sir! Good sir!" I say louder and Biggie scoots in.

I rub the old man's shoulder to get his attention, but he doesn't react. Biggie tries squeezing his thigh lightly. It's as if we don't exist.

"Why? Why?" he continues.

Abbas raises his hands and shakes his head profusely. He starts to cry. I take the water bottle and raise it to his mouth. He stops crying long enough to take a sip, then starts up again. "Why? Why?"

I look at Mike. "You want to give it a try?"

"No," he says. "You're doing a great job."

I shake my head. Mike turns to Abbas. "Hey, you! Abbas! Look at me!"

Mike snaps his fingers in the old man's face, but Abbas pays him no attention.

"Why? Why?"

"Look at me!" Mike yells.

We don't exist. Biggie looks for direction.

"Taxi time?" I say.

"Roger that," Mike says.

Twenty minutes later we pull out of the main gate in our SUV with Biggie and Abbas in back. We weave between the Jersey barriers and stop where the road leads to the city. There's a line of taxis in the distance and one starts up and approaches. Biggie gets Abbas out of the car and puts a stash of money in the front pocket of his dishdasha. The taxi stops in front of us and Biggie carefully puts the old man in the backseat, gives the driver the address, and then pays him an advance fare. The taxi makes a U-turn and pulls away.

In the backseat, Abbas is still asking, "Why? Why?"

9

Round Two

July 2, 2006

There are no World Cup soccer matches scheduled as the four remaining teams—France, Italy, Portugal, and the host country Germany—rest for their semifinal matchups. Mike and I sit in front of our computers. He types an e-mail and I'm watching *Band of Brothers.*

"What are the odds that the phone will ring?" Mike asks.

"One to one," I reply.

I've been in the unit for three weeks and have racked up close to twenty-five missions. We've raided more than thirty homes.

"Care to guess a time?" Mike asks.

"It's impossible to predict," I reply. "It would be futile."

"Then, how about dinner?"

"Sounds good to me," I say.

We peek into the terp den on our way to the SUV and ask if Biggie and Tiny want to join us. They cooked local food for themselves so they pass.

During the drive across the base Mike and I joke about military life. We lament about the poor guy who sits at the front of our compound, whose only job is to raise and lower the barrier arm. He must have pissed someone off.

We discuss the similarities between hunting terrorists and Mike's job as a cop in Texas. When we've encountered screaming wives during our raids, Mike is the first cool head to address them calmly and try to alleviate their fears and complaints. He presents a confident, calm presence in the close quarters of homes where emotions can rage like wildfires. He's taught me a few street-cop tricks of the trade for questioning detainees and I've shared my cultural knowledge of the Middle East. We don't convince everyone to cooperate, but we're close. Little by little we improve our techniques.

Outside the chow hall we clear our pistols, wash our hands in a huge metal trough, step inside, and grab trays. The chow hall is the length of a football field and can seat enough soldiers to fill Lambeau Field. There are two dozen service lines with everything from grilled hamburgers to beef Stroganoff. Two lines are just for desserts. A rock 'n' roll band plays at the center of the chow hall. It's a circus. Rows upon rows of long tables seat soldiers hurriedly gulping down plates piled high with food. We pass soldiers with uniforms of a strange camouflage pattern and I recognize the patch on the sleeve. It's an Albanian flag. *There are Albanians in Iraq?* I think. As I wait for my grilled chicken and pasta, a memory returns.

Seven years ago, as a pilot I was in charge of planning special operations helicopter missions during the conflict in Kosovo. I computed flight paths, fuel loads, and weapons configurations. I scheduled air crews and coordinated flights as part of the Joint Special Operations Task Force stationed at San Vito Air Station, Italy. Once the war kicked off, operations quickly escalated to high gear. I worked incessantly, sleeping just four hours a night on a couch. There was never enough time to do all the tasks the job required.

A few weeks into the war, my commander approached me with an important tasking. Thousands of ethnic Albanians were fleeing the genocide in Kosovo over the border and into northern Albania and they desperately needed food. My mission was to coordinate helicopter airlift of food aid from Tirana, the Albanian capital, to the refugee camps.

The next day I boarded a two-ship helicopter formation and headed to Tirana. Together with another pilot, I attended a NATO meeting to discuss helicopter flights to supply food aid to the refugees. An hour later, as the Europeans pettily argued over which side of the valley to fly on, we walked out, loaded up our helicopters with food, and flew it up to the camps. We landed in a soccer field and as soon as we shut down the rotors, the helicopters were swarmed by hundreds of newly orphaned kids. They snatched every patch, pen, and object on my flight suit or in my pockets. I brought a soccer ball that I had bought at the BX and kicked it into the crowd. We unloaded the food and returned to Tirana for more. By the time we landed back at Tirana after our third trip, the NATO meeting was breaking up. We made a last run and headed home.

That was not our only accomplishment. In addition to conducting dozens of special operations missions, my unit, the 21st Special Operations Squadron, also brought back the Stealth pilot who was shot down behind enemy lines and an F-16 pilot who bailed out over enemy territory when his engine quit.

Mike and I take our seats at a table amidst strangers.

"Are you anxious to get home?" I ask.

"I miss the wife and daughter," Mike replies.

"How old is she?"

"She just started talking."

I chose Mike for this job on the raid team when I was the senior interrogator back at the main prison. I knew he wanted it and I was happy to help him get it, but I can't help but feel a little anxiety over the fact that he would be a lot safer back at the main prison, where we never went outside the wire. The biggest threat back there was the daily mortar attacks. It is a credit to Mike that he volunteered to come here. I'm sure the tactical aspects of the mission appealed to a former SWAT sniper.

"What's the first thing you are going to do when you get home?" I ask.

"Hold my daughter," he says. "What about you?"

"Surf," I reply.

"Seriously?"

"Don't get me wrong, I miss my family, but after all this sand and no water, I need to ride a wave."

The rock 'n' roll band starts up and the music echoes throughout the chow hall.

"It's like G. I. Disney," I say.

"In two days it will be the Fourth of July," Mike replies.

"I almost forgot."

That's the way the days go in Iraq. Your head swirls in obsession with your mission, and everything back in the normal world fades. Friends, family, hobbies—they all become blurred memories . . . until you come home. Then, sooner or later, the enormity of it all hits you.

Interrogators rarely talk among themselves about the stresses of the job. It's taboo. But imagine holding the fates of people's lives in your hands day in and day out for months on end. An infantryman sees a target and shoots it. He never has to get to know the target, learn about his wife and children, get to know him as a fellow member of the human race. He doesn't have to listen to his hardships. The target is just a bad guy. The infantryman doesn't have to deal with feeling empathy for his enemy after he hears about his mother's illness. Good interrogators are burdened with the emotional toll of living through the experiences of everyone who sits down in front of them. An experienced interrogator will put himself in the shoes of every detainee he interrogates, feel what the detainee feels, and then leverage that knowledge. It's mentally and emotionally draining. And sometimes things go wrong.

Interrogators make mistakes. You are sure your detainee is being truthful and it turns out he is lying. Based on the false information elicited, you send a team out on a mission. Maybe they get hit by a roadside bomb. Maybe a soldier is killed by suicide bombers. Maybe they raid the wrong house and shoot an Iraqi mother of three. Maybe an innocent twelve-year-old boy ends up in a body bag. It happens. We lost two pilots during a mission to attack a target my team developed when I was at the main prison. Two damn good men.

A shooter can mistakenly shoot the wrong target and walk away with a clear conscience as long as he followed protocol. But an interrogator will forever second-guess himself and wonder if he didn't miss a clue that the detainee was lying. Or ponder if he could have gotten just one more detail that would have saved lives.

Interrogators are actors on the world's most notorious stage. Even when things go awry, we hide our emotions from each other and press on with our jobs. We are professionals and we are proud of our work. But there are costs when we're back stateside.

Mike and I return to our office with full stomachs and take seats behind our desks. Just as I click the play button on my computer, the Bat Phone rings. Mike answers.

" 'Gators," he says. "Yup, got it."

Before he can hang up the phone I'm out of my chair.

We take the same route back to Hamza's house and everything looks the same from outside the porthole, except the world is seen through black-and-green night-vision. We pass my "favorite," and only, Kirkuk garbage can.

Outside the home a semitrailer is parked. The raid goes uneventfully and inside the house we capture Abbas (again) and Abu Hamza, Hamza's father. Hamza is not home even though his truck is parked out front. Mike goes to the utility room to question the wife and kids while I approach the father, standing in the family room.

Abu Hamza is stocky, with thick black hair and a large nose. He wears a white dishdasha.

"As-salamu alaykum," I say.

"Alaykum as-salam."

His hands are flexi-cuffed behind his back and he stands against the wall with his chest sticking out. He inspects me as the soldiers around us search his home. Biggie translates.

"What is your name?"

"Abu Hamza."

"What is your work?"

"I don't have work now," he replies.

"Why not?"

"My business is finished. I had a clothing store."

"I'm sorry to hear that," I say. "It must be difficult to feed your family."

He nods lightly.

"Where is your son?"

"My son has done nothing," he replies.

"I didn't say that he did anything wrong. I just want to talk to him."

"Why?"

"I think he might know somebody."

"My son is not involved with the terrorists."

I turn to Biggie. "Did he say *terrorists*?"

"Yes," Biggie replies.

I turn back to Abu Hamza. "I just want to talk to him. When will he be back?"

"I don't know."

"Where is he?"

"He went to Baghdad."

"Why Baghdad?"

"He didn't say."

"You have no idea why he went to Baghdad?"

Abu Hamza sticks out his chest a little farther. "He is not involved with the terrorists!"

"I didn't say that he was," I reply. "I just want to talk to him."

"I don't know when he will be back."

The Alabama Lieutenant taps me on the shoulder. I turn around and he whispers, "I don't want to be here too long."

"Roger that," I say. "Let's take him back to the base. The old man can stay."

In the utility room, the wife starts yelling. Mike enters with Tiny and joins our circle.

"She knows we're going to take her husband and she's pissed," Mike says.

"He won't tell us the location of Hamza, so we have no choice," I reply.

Abu Hamza's wife appears in the doorway and a soldier blocks her path. She yells at us over him. It needs no translation. I can imagine what she's saying.

"She's angry that you are taking her husband," Biggie says.

"Nothing I can do about that," I say. "He won't cooperate. Load him up."

The Lieutenant nods and we retreat to the Strykers.

"I'm not going to harm your son," I say. "I just want to ask him some questions."

Abu Hamza sits in a white plastic chair in the interrogation room. His arms are crossed in front of his chest and he wears a scowl.

"Why do you keep bothering us?" he asks. "We have done nothing wrong."

"I just need to talk to your son," I repeat.

"He is not involved."

"Your wife told me that he drives to Iran to deliver goods."

"Yes, that is true."

"I just want to ask him who he knows in Iran. Maybe I can help him and he can help me."

"He doesn't need help. He has a good job. He doesn't make trouble."

"I know," I say. "He's not in trouble."

"I cannot help you," Abu Hamza says.

"Did I harm your brother? All we did was ask him questions."

"He is an old man. You should not have taken him from my home."

"I apologize for that," I say. "I didn't know at the time. I gave him money, no? I gave your wife money."

Abu Hamza stares in silence.

Trust is the fundamental building block of any interrogation and Abu Hamza does not trust me. Even though we treated his brother with care and gave his family money, he still doesn't trust us. There's a reason why and we both know what it is: Abu Ghraib. Guantanamo Bay. Our looking the other way when the Shi'a militias conducted reprisal killings across Iraq. We have lost the confidence of the Sunnis in Iraq and have a long way to go to regain it. Words will not suffice. It will take action.

This is a significant negative consequence of the torture and abuse sanctioned by the United States government following the start of the war. It puts every interrogator at a disadvantage when they start an interview. Detainees see every interrogator as a torturer. Even if torture was effective—and there's plenty of evidence to suggest it's not 99.99 percent of the time—the short-term gains will never outweigh the long-term consequences. I met many Iraqis who liked Americans and enjoyed our culture, but all that changed after our war crimes were exposed. It will take a tremendous effort to regain ground, and the first step is accountability.

That said, one of my biggest surprises in Iraq is how far an apology can go. Back at the main prison, an apology for America's mistakes in Iraq followed by an offer to work together in the future convinced several high-ranking members of al Qaeda to cooperate. The Sunnis in Iraq are moderates—they like Americans, but they see us favoring the Shi'a. To understand the political realities of Iraq, one only has to look at a map and the location of Iraq's oil fields. There is oil in the predominant Shi'a lands to the east and south, and in the Kurdish territory to the north, but there is none in Sunni-dominated lands. The Sunnis realize all too well that in a democratic Iraq where they will always be outvoted two to one, they have a very narrow political avenue to access future oil revenues—unless they resort to violence. Our policy of favoring the Shi'a and de-Baathification pushed Iraqi Sunnis right into the hands of al Qaeda. It's my job as an interrogator to bring them back to our side. The chips are stacked against me, but it starts with an apology, and then an offer.

"Look," I say to Abu Hamza, "I'm sorry we keep coming to your house. I don't want to have to keep returning, but I need to talk to your son. To show good faith, today I will release you."

"I'm going home?" he asks.

"Yes, I'm going to let you go and I'm going to give you some money. I apologize for the inconvenience, but you have to realize that I have a job to do. I need to talk to your son."

"He is not involved," Abu Hamza says.

"Very well," I say, "let's go."

Biggie and I load Abu Hamza into the back of the SUV and drive him out the front gate. We leave him at the end of the Jersey barriers and wave for a taxi. As we're waiting for the taxi to pull up, I hand Abu Hamza a roll of cash. He puts it into his pocket and without a word I climb back into the SUV.

Abu Hamza climbs into the taxi and as it pulls a U-turn, he throws a dark stare.

"See you tomorrow," I say.

Father and Son

The son of a duck is a floater.   **—Arab Proverb**

July 3, 2006

With the sun directly overhead we pass my favorite garbage can, again. When we pull up to the house, the semitrailer is gone and Abu Hamza is waiting for us in the doorway. The door is missing. Apparently, despite the money we've compensated him, he's sick of repairing it. He invites the soldiers inside and they awkwardly scramble past him and through the house, unaccustomed to such cordiality. The last soldier in line grabs Abu Hamza and pulls him inside, quickly securing his hands behind his back. Once the house is secure, we are called in.

Abu Hamza stands once again in his living room with his hands flexi-cuffed. His warm welcoming didn't make him immune to security precautions. Mike and Tiny head for the utility room to question Abu Hamza's wife and kids. I owe them one.

I greet Abu Hamza, pull my shears from my medical pouch, and free his hands. He rubs at his wrists as I invite him to sit next to me on the couch. Biggie sits opposite us on a blue velvet recliner.

"I told you that I would be back," I say.

"You are a man of your word," he replies with a smile.

"I don't want to keep coming here."

"There is nothing I can do."

The soldiers search the house all around us, upending furniture and emptying drawers onto the floor. They are not happy about returning to the same house three times. The voice of Abu Hamza's wife echoes in the background.

"We could keep doing this," I say. "I have plenty of time."

"So do I," Abu Hamza replies.

A soldier accidentally drops a drawer and the contents spill onto the floor.

"This is not safe for us," I say. "I have to risk the roadside bombs to get here."

"That is your choice."

The Alabama Lieutenant enters the room and raises his eyebrows. I shake my head negatively.

"Let's go, then," he says, "I don't want to stay here. We're establishing a pattern."

"Give me a few more minutes," I ask.

"Forget about it," he says. "You've already talked to him. Obviously, he is not going to help us."

I rise from the couch and nod toward the door. The Lieutenant follows me outside. We bake in the hot sun.

"I can convince him to turn in his son," I say.

"Turn in his son?" the Lieutenant answers. "Impossible! No Iraqi is going to do that!"

"I'm just asking for five more minutes."

The Lieutenant mulls it over. Mike and I have established a reputation for getting results and now I'm cashing in.

"Okay, five minutes. But then we're out of here."

"Agreed," I say.

I return to the room and pull Biggie to the side.

"Can you write your cell-phone number down on a piece of paper?" I ask.

"Sure," Biggie says and I hand him my notepad and pen.

He scribbles the number on a piece of paper and I shove it into my pocket. I return to the couch next to Abu Hamza while Biggie takes his place on the recliner.

"No need to stay," Abu Hamza says.

I smile. "Did I treat you well when you came to the base?"

"Yes," he replies.

"What about your brother?"

"Yes."

"Have I insulted you in any way?"

"No."

"Did I treat you with respect?"

"Yes."

"I will do the same for your son. I just want to ask him some questions."

Abu Hamza inspects my face.

"Thank you for coming," he says.

I stand up and put out my hand. He takes it and I pass the piece of paper with Biggie's number.

"What's this?" he asks.

"Take care," I say and turn for the door.

July 4, 2006

It's *Top Gun* with tattoos. Shirtless men in dark sunglasses stand on either side of the volleyball net. Beside the court, rows of burgers and dogs burn on a grill. Nearby, picnic tables are loaded with chips, condiments, and two-liter bottles of soda.

"Before you start," Templeton says with a smile from his position at the side of the court, "I want you all to know that you should enjoy your day off because it's the only one you're going to get."

The court erupts in laughter. Even Templeton is in a festive mood.

Mike and I sit at a picnic bench with Biggie and Tiny, enjoying the food. We sip Cokes from red plastic cups.

"Finally, a day off," Mike says. "How long have we been here?"

"About three and a half months," I reply.

I can't complain. I love it here in the north with the raid team. It's such a welcome relief compared to the *Groundhog Day* atmosphere of the main prison. The days are just as long, if not longer, and the risk is significantly greater, but there is also more freedom. We are slaves to the Bat Phone, but after a mission and the ensuing interrogations, sometimes there's a short break in which we can relax. We can even sneak in an episode of *The Shield* or a World Cup game.

"Who do you think will win the game tonight?" I ask the terps.

"Germany for sure," Tiny says. "They have home field advantage."

"Germany," Biggie agrees. "Their goalkeeper is the best."

"Mike?" I ask.

"How the hell would I know?" he says. "I only started watching soccer a few weeks ago."

"What about you?" Tiny asks.

"I'm rooting for Italy," I say, "with respect for my ancestors."

"You're about as Italian as a cheeseburger," Mike quips.

"Cheers to that," I say and raise my plastic cup.

Biggie's cell phone rings and he answers it. "Hello?"

He switches to Arabic and has a quick exchange. Suddenly, his voice grows excited.

"Okay, okay," he ends and hangs up the phone.

"What?" I ask.

Biggie's eyes are as large as Frisbees. "That was Abu Hamza. He's at the front gate with his son."

I nearly drop my cup.

"Holy shit!" Tiny says.

"Unbelievable," Mike manages.

"I'll drive," I say.

We jump from the table. As I pass Templeton standing next to the volleyball court he calls to me.

"Where are you headed in such a hurry?"

"To pick up Hamza," I reply.

"What?" he says.

"I'll tell you when I get back," I yell over my shoulder.

Abu Hamza stands on the side of the road just past the Jersey barriers with his son. Hamza is the younger, spitting image of his father, except he has bright blue eyes. He wears a white dishdasha. I park the SUV twenty yards away. Mike and I have SIG Sauers and our body armor, but no helmets. Biggie has on his body armor. We inspect the scene for a minute before exiting the vehicle. I greet Abu Hamza.

"My friend, *as-salamu alaykum.*"

"*Alaykum as-salam,*" Abu Hamza replies.

As I approach, he raises his head and there are tears in his eyes. He holds his son's hand. Hamza stands half a foot taller than his father, steady and unafraid.

"Good to see you again," I say.

"Good to see you," he replies.

His hands start to shake. Mike steps forward and grabs Hamza by the arm. Suddenly, Abu Hamza pulls at his son's hand.

"No! No!" Abu Hamza yells. "You cannot!"

"It's okay, my friend, it's okay," I say.

I take a step forward and put my hand on Abu Hamza's shoulder. Biggie steps between father and son and also lends a hand, rubbing Abu Hamza's other shoulder.

Tears flow down Abu Hamza's face and his expression turns to anger.

"No!" he yells as he loses hold of his son's hand.

Mike quickly leads Hamza toward the vehicle and opens the back door. Hamza willingly gets inside and Mike shuts it.

"Please!" Abu Hamza yells. "Please!"

"I will take care of him," I say. "I promise."

I nod to Biggie and he gives the father a last squeeze of the shoulder and retreats. We get into the SUV and I turn the ignition and put the vehicle in drive. As we pull away I catch a last glimpse of Abu Hamza, standing on the side of the road, crying. He raises his hands to the sky and shouts:

"Why? Why?"

His voice fades in the distance as I weave through the Jersey barriers and back onto the base.

Hamza sits comfortably in his chair in the interrogation room. Mike and Tiny sit to the side. Like always, it's a sauna.

"How often do you drive to Iran?" Mike asks through Tiny.

"Twice a month," Hamza replies. He answers with a slow wave of the hand.

"Where in Iran?" Mike asks.

"Many different cities. I go wherever my boss sends me."

"What is the name of your boss?"

"Nasim."

No dice. Hamza is linked to our next target—Walid.

"Where does Nasim live?"

"I don't know. I've only seen him at my home."

"Your home? You've never been to his office?"

"No. Never. He only comes to my home."

"I don't believe it," Mike says. "He doesn't have an office?"

"Yes, he does," Hamza answers. "But I've never been there."

"Where is the office?" Mike asks.

"There's a truck yard near the edge of town."

"How did you get your truck?" Mike asks.

"He drove it to my home."

"When was that?"

"About a year ago. That was when he hired me."

"Can you show me the location of the truck yard on a map?"

"Yes," Hamza agrees.

Mike pulls out a map of Kirkuk from his pocket. He shows it to Hamza, noting the location of Hamza's house. Hamza orients himself quickly and then traces a highway with his finger to the outskirts of town.

"Here," he points. "This is the truck yard."

Mike marks the spot with a Sharpie.

"What hours does he work?" Mike continues.

"I heard he is there every day, but I don't know for sure because I've never been."

"What kinds of goods do you transport?"

"Mostly food items," Hamza answers. "Produce, meat, rice. Sometimes tea."

"Do you have trouble getting across the border?"

"No, there is no problem."

Mike and I are thinking the same thing. The intel guys believe that the Iranians are helping al Qaeda to build Explosively Formed Projectiles, the advanced form of roadside bomb that can penetrate thick steel. It's the type of IED that hit the Stryker in front of us just a couple of weeks ago.

"Have you ever carried weapons?" Mike asks.

"No," Hamza replies. "Never."

"People?"

"No."

"Really?" Mike says, raising his voice. "How do you know Abu Azir?"

"I don't know anyone by that name," Hamza replies and crosses his arms on his chest.

"Then explain this," Mike says and hands Hamza the list we recovered from Abu Azir.

Hamza cautiously takes the list from Mike and reads it. His blue eyes stop on his name and address.

"Why would your name and address be on this list?"

Hamza looks up at Mike and then back at the list.

"I don't know," he responds. "I've never heard of this man."

"So it's all just a coincidence?" Mike yells. "You just *happen* to be on the same list as ten other members of al Qaeda?!"

"I don't know about any of this," Hamza says.

"Bullshit!" Mike yells.

From under my chair I grab a brown file filled with papers, and show it to him.

"Look," I say calmly, "we have all this information about you and this cell. We know about Abu Azir and

Omar and Walid. We know that Abu Azir sells weapons. Hell, we have them next door in our evidence room. Do you want to see them?"

"No," Hamza replies.

He looks down again at the list of names. Mike reaches over and grabs it from him. I wave the heavy file in front of Hamza. One page sticks out beyond the edges.

"Do you think we would have spent all this time compiling information and going to your house three times if we didn't already know that you transport weapons from Iran for Abu Azir?"

One of the pieces of paper slips out of the file as I wave it and falls on the floor. It's Abu Azir's mug shot. Hamza glances down at the photo as I pick it up. I tuck it back into the file, among the dozens of blank pages that he cannot see, and place the file back under my chair.

"We have enough information on you already," I say. "We don't need anymore. The fact is, my fingers are tired from all the typing."

"Me too," Mike adds. "What my partner is saying is that we want to burn your file."

"Burn?" Hamza asks.

"Yes, burn it. We don't need you. We need Walid."

"I don't know Walid," he replies.

Mike turns to me. "He's listening to us but he's not hearing us. He doesn't want us to help him."

Tiny continues to translate the conversation. He knows our routine.

"I know!" I shout. "It's so frustrating! We're trying to help him but he won't let us!"

"You offer him an olive branch and he refuses it!" Mike adds. "It's insulting!"

"This is no way to treat hosts! We treated his father and his uncle with respect and we gave his family money!"

"I know!" Mike continues the charade. "I thought we were friends! Here we are helping him and his family and he won't do the same for us!"

Hamza unfolds his arms and tries to talk but I interrupt him.

"I know . . . I know!" I yell. "You're going to say that you *are* trying to help but you don't know Walid! You don't know Abu Azir! You don't know how your name magically appeared on this list! You don't know about all the information in the file!"

Hamza tries to reply again, but Mike cuts him off.

"Right! Let me guess—you want us to help you but you don't want to help us. You want to go home to see your father? The same father that brought you here because he trusts us? How come your father trusts us so much that he brought you here but you won't give us the same courtesy?"

"Exactly!" I say. "Your father is a man of honor! He is

a man that respects other honest men! He knows that the admirable thing to do is to tell the truth!"

"I admire your father!" Mike says. "Look at the amount of courage it took to work with us! I mean, we've made some mistakes in Iraq, but he was willing to forgive us and give us a second chance because he saw that we showed him respect!"

"Right!" I say. "We should show respect when we reach out to each other! We should work together and help each other!"

"We are all trying to make Iraq a safer place!" Mike says. Then his voice fades to almost a whisper as he repeats, "We are all just trying to make Iraq a safer place."

I nod my head in agreement and Mike hangs his, exhausted and frustrated and deserving of an Emmy. Even Tiny joins in and shakes his head in disbelief that Hamza won't work with us. After a moment of silence, Hamza is the first to speak.

"I thank you for helping my family," he says, "but I cannot help you."

"Why not?" Mike asks.

"Because I do not want to kill my family."

Realization sets in. Hamza believes that if he cooperates with us, al Qaeda will retaliate.

"No one needs to know that you are helping us," Mike says.

"I'm sorry," Hamza replies, "but I cannot help."

I wonder if our compassion is not weaker than al Qaeda's hate. The old school of interrogators would say that a man like Hamza only understands fear and violence. They would say that a man who transports weapons for al Qaeda, weapons that take the lives of innocent civilians, cannot be persuaded with niceties. They argue that my methods are a waste of time. They are wrong.

Leveraging the best of our culture—tolerance, cultural understanding, intellect, ingenuity, and, yes, compassion—gives us the best possibility of success, but it's never a sure thing. Doctors can't cure all patients and infantrymen don't shoot every target. And that's okay. It's times like this, when we encounter obstacles, that we have to regroup, assess our tactics, and improve them.

Our approach is a good one. It's called the "File and Dossier" combined with the "We Know All" in the Army Field Manual, but tailored with a deep understanding of Arab culture. We mixed in the concept of respect and an Arab cultural obligation to help those who help you. We chose this approach based on our knowledge of Hamza's father, believing that Hamza would have inherited some of his father's traits. But there's an unintended consequence—our emphasis on respect includes Hamza's respect for his father and his family, and that includes protecting them. That's what I think is going on in his head, but I don't know for sure.

Mike and I continue interrogating Hamza for another two hours. We go in circles. We try several other approaches, but he continues to insist that he must protect his family. In the end, Mike and I put Hamza in a cell and walk back to our office.

"He's a tough nut to crack," Mike says.

"Yeah, his argument is a difficult one to overcome," I say.

"We offered to try and protect his family."

"But he knows that we can't. How many times have we actually gone out and moved a family? Not since I've been here."

"I wish there was a program to do that," Mike says.

"Maybe they'll come up with one," I reply.

Mike turns on the television. The World Cup game between Italy and Germany is in overtime and the score is zero to zero. In the one hundred eighteenth minute, Italy scores twice consecutively, wins the game, and earns a spot in the final.

"You called that one," Mike says.

"Not really," I say. "I was rooting for them but I thought they would lose. It just goes to show, there's always hope."

There are explosions outside and we leave the office to investigate. Fireworks fill the night sky with bright colors and streams of light.

"Happy Fourth of July," Mike says.

July 4, 2006 (Night)

Jeff sits behind his desk in the command post, typing on his computer.

"What's up?" he says without looking up.

"Hamza says that he works for a man named Nasim," I say. "He has an office at a truck yard on the outskirts of town."

"Do you think Nasim and Walid are one and the same?" Jeff asks as he looks up from his computer.

"He wouldn't have given him up so easily if he was involved in the weapons shipments," Mike says, "but we're going to interrogate him again in the morning. Maybe we'll get more then."

"Too late," Jeff says. "Hamza's boarding a plane for the main facility now."

"Already?" I ask.

"They wanted him down there quickly because of his ties to Iran."

"Bigger fish across the border?" Mike asks.

"The Iranian connection is a hot priority," Jeff says. "Who knows what might heat up over there?"

Mike and I exchange a concerned look. Everyone who comes to Iraq feels the strain of fighting two wars at once. The possibility of a third is unimaginable.

"Back to Nasim," I say. "We could grab him and if he's

not Walid, then maybe we can get him to tell us where to find him."

"I like the idea," Jeff says, "plus Templeton will like it. This team leaves in two days and he wants at least one more capture. Plus, a dozen bodies were found in the streets today with bullet holes in their heads. Mahmoud isn't slowing down."

The door to the command post opens and Templeton walks in to join our gathering.

"Gentlemen, what's up?" he asks.

Jeff explains the intelligence.

"You have anything else to confirm that Nasim might be Walid?" he asks Jeff.

Jeff rubs his hand across the top of his shaved head.

"Nothing, sir," he says. "We're looking for a Walid and the address on the list is nowhere close to the truck yard."

"But the address on the list might be his home," Mike adds, "or just a safehouse."

"We've had some guys looking at the home address," Templeton replies. "It's empty."

"I'm sure as soon as we raided Abu Azir's house, word went out," I say. "We were lucky to get Hamza."

"It was our luck that he still lived with his parents," Jeff says. "Maybe he didn't get word because he was in Iran."

Templeton scratches at his chin and turns to Jeff.

"Have any other targets developed?"

"None, sir," Jeff answers.

"Then we launch on the truck yard in thirty minutes. Make the call."

"Yes, sir," Jeff says.

Templeton turns to us. "You know, I didn't have much faith in you 'gators when you arrived, but I have to hand it to you. Now I trust your information more than any other source."

He walks over to his desk and sits down in front of his computer while Mike and I head for the office to put on our gear.

All Roads Lead to Mecca

July 5, 2006

The night air is cool on my face and the truck yard comes into view. We prepared ourselves before our arrival with satellite imagery that showed that the truck yard is a quarter-mile triangular plot of land bordered on two sides by major roads. There are two office buildings on site and the team plans to hit them simultaneously. In the imagery, the lot was filled with semitrailers, truck parts, and huge rows of tires.

Our formation slows at the main gate to make the turn. As we enter, the formation splits in two and races to the offices. Our Stryker stops just inside the main entrance and we wait for the call. Within minutes it comes over the radio and we pull forward between rows of parked semitrailers to one of the offices. Outside the entrance, an old man in plaid pajamas is sitting on the ground, hands flexi-cuffed. The Lieutenant is standing over him as we approach.

"We captured this guy inside sleeping on a cot," the Lieutenant says.

"Roger," I say. "We'll talk to him."

I kneel down in front of the old man with Biggie. Mike and Tiny stand behind us, waiting.

"As-salamu alaykum," I say.

"Alaykum as-salam," he replies weakly.

The skin on his face sags.

"What is your name?" I ask.

"Talib," he answers.

"Talib, what is your job here?"

"I am the night-shift manager."

"Who is your boss?"

"My boss is Nasim."

"Is Nasim here?"

"No, we haven't seen or heard from him in a week."

"Do you know where he is?"

"No."

"Do you know where he lives?"

"No. I have never been to his house."

"Does he have any relatives working here?"

"I don't know. I've only been here for a week."

The old man looks up with bloodshot eyes.

"Please," he says, "I am only the night manager. Please don't take me to prison. I have to feed my family."

I put a hand on Talib's shoulder.

"Don't worry, my friend," I reassure him. "We are not taking you anywhere."

"Hamdullilah," he replies.

Thanks be to Allah.

"No problem," I say. "Look, just help me out a little bit, okay?"

"Anything," the old man says. "Just don't take me to prison."

"What type of car does Nasim drive?"

"He has a white Mercedes."

"New one?"

"No, I think it is older. It is a sedan."

"When is the last time you saw him?"

"One week ago. That was the day he hired me. He gave me a key to the office and told me to watch over the lot at night."

"Do you have security guards?"

"We don't need them. I have a shotgun under my cot, but nobody steals from Nasim."

"Why not?"

"I don't want to say that."

Biggie and I share a thought with an exchanged look. Mike has been eavesdropping and he kneels down beside me.

"Is there anyone else on the lot that knows Nasim?" he asks.

"I'm not sure," Talib answers.

"What about the other office?" Mike asks.

"That one is used only for sleeping. Nobody works there."

The Lieutenant's radio crackles and he speaks into his mouthpiece. "Roger, we'll send one of them over."

He nods at me.

"You take this," I say to Mike.

"Got it," he replies.

Biggie and I walk with the Lieutenant across the bone-yard of semitrailers. Trucks in varying states of decay are parked in long rows. It's completely quiet.

We arrive at the other office and sitting on the ground are two middle-aged men with their hands flexi-cuffed. The Lieutenant leaves us to do our jobs and I greet the captured men.

"What are your names?" I ask.

"Rami," one answers.

"Latif," the other one replies.

"Do you work here?"

"We are just truckers," Rami answers. "We were only sleeping."

The second trucker, in his midthirties, remains silent.

"Who is your boss?" I ask.

"Nasim," Rami replies.

"When did you last see Nasim?" I ask.

"About one week ago. No one has seen him since.

That's why we are sleeping here. We are waiting for him to come back and give us work."

"Do you know where he went?" I ask.

"No," Rami says.

"What about you?" Biggie asks.

"I've never met him," Latif answers.

"Where are you from?" Biggie asks.

"Syria."

"Do you have a passport?" Biggie asks.

"No," Latif replies.

"You are here illegally?"

"Yes."

Biggie translates the conversation for me.

"Do you think he is involved or just an illegal truck driver looking for work?" I ask.

"I don't know," Biggie says. "There are so many foreigners in Iraq causing trouble."

Biggie doesn't share his opinions of the war. I'm sure that he's happy to have a Shi'a government in power in Iraq and especially happy that Saddam is gone, but I don't know his true feelings about the Shi'a militias. Does he quietly root for the Badr Corps or the Mahdi Army? I doubt the latter, but al-Sistani's Army is supported by a politically moderate Shi'a majority that has captured the majority of government offices. Also, al-Sistani has close ties to Iran.

Now that sanctions have been lifted, there are hundreds of foreigners driving trucks filled with cargo across

Iraq's borders. Hence the kidnap victim that arrived at our main prison to whom I gave money a couple months ago. He was Syrian and had been driving from Damascus to Baghdad along the western highway when he was kidnapped at an insurgent roadblock. The kidnappers shot two truckers on the spot and took the Syrian and his friend captive. They held them for ransom while they extorted their trucking companies. When the other trucker's company paid the ransom, the kidnappers dragged him outside the house where they were being held and shot him in the head. The Syrian trucker we rescued was held for three months, during which time he was regularly beaten and tortured. He feared the same end as the other trucker, but it was his fate to be rescued by Americans.

I turn to the Syrian. "How long have you been in Iraq?"

"One week," he says.

"What are you doing here?"

"I want to drive a cargo truck," he says. "In Syria there are no jobs."

"Have you done this before?" I ask.

"Yes, many times."

"Why Iraq?"

"Because Americans have given the Iraqis a lot of money," he says. "They are rich."

American reconstruction money has filled the pockets

of savvy Iraqi businessmen, and legitimate foreigners have flocked to Iraq not only to join al Qaeda, but to also earn prized dollars.

The Lieutenant approaches. "Got anything?"

"No, nothing," I reply. "They are saying the same thing as the old man. Nasim was last seen a week ago and no one knows where he is or when he is coming back."

"Should we bring them back to the base?"

"I don't think so," I say. "We're not going to get much more out of them and I'm not sure they are involved."

"Roger," he says. "Then let's load up."

I pull out my shears and cut the flexi-cuffs from the men's hands. They rub at their wrists. Biggie and I walk back across the truck lot toward our Stryker.

"It's not easy," I say to him, "distinguishing between the good and bad foreigners."

"These foreigners come to Iraq and cause trouble," he says.

"Throughout its history, Iraq has hosted many foreigners," I reply.

"They come and go," Biggie says.

"It's strange, isn't it?" I ask. "The great warrior, Saladin, lived here in Kirkuk. Maybe at one time he stood here on this piece of land."

"Iraq has a long history."

"The birth of civilization," I reply.

"Let's hope this is not the end of it," Biggie says.

July 6, 2006

"Dry hole," I say to Templeton.

Outside the command post the day's first light is filtering over the horizon.

"Damn," Templeton says.

"Sir, we're working another angle," Jeff says. "We might be able to pinpoint him through other means."

Templeton turns to Jeff. "How long do you think?"

"Maybe another day or two," Jeff replies.

"It's too long," Templeton says. "I want that son of a bitch Mahmoud and we only have two days left."

"Technically, we only have one," the Lieutenant says, raising his watch.

The digital face reads 0600. Except for a twenty-minute nap, I have been up for forty-eight hours straight.

"Roger," Templeton says. "Stand the guys down for seven hours. After that, we go back on alert."

"Yes, sir," the Lieutenant says.

Back at the office, I give Mike the news.

"Seven hours," he repeats. "Are you going to sleep?"

"I'm too wired."

"Me too. We should go to the Doc and get Ambien."

"My sleep cycle is so messed up, that's probably a great idea."

184

We retreat to our trailers and take showers. Then we walk over to the Doc's office to get Ambien.

"Take one and make sure you get six hours of uninterrupted sleep," he instructs.

I return to my room—one-third of a trailer. My predecessor taped cardboard over the only window so that it's a black box. The air-conditioning unit on the wall hums quietly. I take the Ambien and lay down in bed for my six hours of uninterrupted sleep. I'm out instantly. Suddenly, someone is pounding on my door. In the darkness, I stumble across the room and crack it open. The sunlight is blinding and I can't make out the young soldier standing on the step.

"You're needed at the command post," he says.

"Okay," I reply, "I'll be there in a minute."

I shut the door and turn on the light. I stumble around as I pull on a pair of pants, a shirt, and my sunglasses. I exit the trailer into the hot sun. As I walk through the trailers on the mushy pebbles, I lose my balance and almost fall. I steady myself and try to focus. The world is a blur. I barely make it to the command post and open the door. Everything goes black. I wake up.

I'm in my trailer lying in bed. I walk across the room and turn on the light. I remember walking to the command post and try to recall what happened. My mind is a complete blank. I get dressed, brush my teeth, and walk over to the command post. I ask around, but no one remembers seeing me earlier. I walk back to our office and find Mike behind his desk. I share the story with him and he says he knows nothing about it.

"Maybe you dreamed it all," Mike says.

"But it was so real," I say.

"Well, hopefully they didn't ask you anything important."

"I'll never know."

Mike turns on the television. Portugal and France have just kicked off in a semifinal matchup. The French pull off a 1–0 victory and as a stunned Cristiano Ronaldo shakes hands with the French players, the Bat Phone rings. Mike answers.

" 'Gators."

A voice on the other end.

"Okay . . . roger," he says and hangs up.

"Strykers in ten minutes?" I ask.

"Guess who's talking?"

"No idea," I reply.

"Hamza."

Never dismiss the value of traditional interrogation methods. Our fellow interrogators back at the main prison convinced Hamza to talk and he provided a possible location for Nasim. He said he also goes by the name Walid. There was a Walid on the list we captured from Abu Azir, but the addresses don't match. Missions like these are long shots, but when you turn up a rock, sometimes you find ants.

July 6, 2006 (Night)

"Lock and load!"

We charge our rifles. Our nighttime formation cruises the route NEBRASKA toward the truck yard. The location of the house Hamza provided is nearby. We arrive at a small residential neighborhood of three-story town-homes. The soldiers pour out of the Strykers and set up on an end unit. The medic pulls on my pant leg; in the distance I hear the soldiers gain entry.

The front door to the house is inside a cramped garage filled with scattered engine parts and an old Toyota sedan on blocks. The concrete floor is covered with oil stains. I step around the car and through the doorway, where broken glass crunches underneath my boots. The Lieutenant is standing in the living room.

"Upstairs," he says. "There are some people on the first floor balcony and more on the roof."

At the top of the stairs, Mike and I split up. I go to the first floor balcony with Biggie. Mike and Tiny continue up the stairs to the roof.

On the balcony there is a soldier guarding two twenty-something females and a toddler. One of the young women stands casually against the balcony while the other sits against the wall with the toddler in her lap. I approach the standing girl.

"Hello," she says in English.

I flip up my night-vision monocle.

"Hello," I reply. "Do you live here?"

"Yes," she says.

"What is your name?"

"Mariam," she replies.

She wears no head scarf and has shoulder-length brown hair parted in the middle. Her eyes are light and she has perfect complexion. She wears a T-shirt over blue jeans and is barefoot. If I didn't know any better, I'd swear she was just another American teenager hanging out at the mall.

"Mariam," I say, "who lives in this house?"

"I live here with my father, sister, brother, and uncle."

"What is your father's name?"

"Abu Sadiq," she replies.

"Is this your brother Sadiq?" I ask, nodding toward the toddler.

"Yes," she answers.

"What is your father's given name?"

"Nasim," she replies.

Bingo. Names themselves are a labyrinth in Iraq. Men have given names, nicknames, and paternal names. This is one reason that our databases have been useless in tracking prisoners, and why several times we came across men whom we didn't realize we had captured previously.

"Is your father home?" I ask.

"No, he's been gone for a week," Mariam replies.

She reaches up to her necklace and swings the charm, a silver heart, along its chain.

"Do you know when he will be back?"

"No, he didn't say."

"Do you know where he went?"

"No."

"What is your father's job?" I ask.

"He owns a trucking company," Mariam replies.

"Is this your sister?" I ask, indicating the woman against the wall with the toddler in her lap.

"No, she is my cousin."

"Who is on the roof?"

"My uncle, Bandar."

"Does he work with your father?"

"No. He works in the garage below, fixing cars."

"Does he know where your father is?"

"My father did not tell anyone where he was going. When I talked to him he was very nervous. Why are you looking for him?"

"I just want to ask him some questions," I reply. "It's not him that we are after. We are looking for someone that he knows."

"My father knows many people because of his business."

"Do you know Hamza? He works for your father."

"No."

"Does your father go by any other names?"

"No."

"Does he have any friends named Walid?"

"No, but I don't meet my father's friends."

"Who is his best friend?"

"His best friend is Mahmoud."

Could this be the same Mahmoud? Our mole gone AWOL, also known as the mysterious Zafar? The man behind these last butchers of Iraq, and target number one?

"Where does Mahmoud live?"

"I don't know. I've never been to his house."

"Does he come here often?"

"Sometimes."

"When was the last time you saw him?"

"A week ago," Mariam replies.

"Describe Mahmoud to me," I say.

"He is very short, brown hair, and a brown beard."

Biggie nods in approval as he translates.

"Does he work with your father?"

"I think he owns trucks. I heard him say once that he goes to Iran."

"Do you know the names of any other friends of your father?"

"No," Mariam replies.

She drops the charm around her neck and chews at a fingernail.

"Where is your mother?" I ask.

"She is on the roof."

"Does she know where your father went?"

"He didn't tell anyone," Mariam says and removes her finger from her mouth.

"No one?"

"Everybody is worried about him. My mother said that Americans were looking for him."

"Why would she think that?"

"I don't know."

"Are there any weapons in this house?"

"No."

"Has your father ever had weapons here?"

"No."

I question Mariam for another five minutes. It goes in circles. She claims not to know the location of her father, when he will return, or anyone who would know.

I leave Mariam and her cousin and brother with a soldier and ascend the stairs to the roof, where two soldiers scan the street. One of the soldiers, a young guy with a baby face, whispers to me, "She's pretty hot, no?"

"I'm sorry?" I say.

"The daughter. On the balcony. You talked to her, right?"

"Yes," I reply.

"She's a hottie," the soldier says.

Someone's been away from home too long. I give a polite grin.

Mike finishes questioning a middle-aged woman and walks over. We stand next to a low wall and look out over the neighborhood.

"You got anything?" I ask.

"Nasim's wife and brother," he replies. "Did you know he goes by the name Abu Sadiq?"

"Yes," I say. "His son, Sadiq, is on the second-floor balcony."

"Roger," Mike says. "Neither his wife nor brother-in-law claims to know his location or when he is coming back."

"Same thing with his daughter. She says he has a friend named Mahmoud and described him as a small guy with brown hair and a brown beard."

"Bingo!" Mike says.

"Right, but she doesn't know where he lives. She claims he was here a week ago."

"Interesting," Mike replies.

"She said that her mother was scared that Americans were looking for her father. The mother must know that he is involved in something."

"Yeah, I went down that road but she's giving up nothing."

"What about the brother, Bandar?"

"He claims that he does not work with Nasim. Says that he is just an engine mechanic and works out of the garage downstairs."

"That's what the daughter says."

"What do you think?" Mike asks.

"I say we take Bandar with us. He might know more."

"I agree."

The Alabama Lieutenant emerges from the entrance to the roof and walks over.

"Anything?" he asks.

"This is the right house," I say, "and we've spoken with the target's wife, brother-in-law, and daughter. They say he left a week ago and no one claims to know his location or when he's coming back."

"No shit," he replies.

"The daughter says that he has a friend named Mahmoud and described the same Mahmoud that we are looking for."

"Hot damn!" the Lieutenant says.

"Yes, but she doesn't know where he lives."

"Well, we've already been to his house and he wasn't home. And if he'd have gone back, we would know."

"Your guys find anything in the house?" I ask.

"No, but the guy we captured up here on the roof had two cell phones under his dishdasha, hidden in his underwear."

"He didn't want to talk about them," Mike says. "He

said that one was his and one was his sister's. That is, Nasim's wife."

I turn to the Lieutenant. "We want to bring him back to the base and continue to question him. Maybe it will jog his memory regarding the whereabouts of Nasim."

"Sounds like a good idea," the Lieutenant answers. "No need to hang around here any longer than we have to."

"We'll load him up," I say.

"I heard the daughter is a real looker," the Lieutenant says as I head for the ladder.

One might conclude this unit is composed of testosterone-driven young men who haven't been around women for months.

"She's attractive," I say, "but not so bright."

"Or clever enough to play stupid," Mike adds.

"Touché," I say.

"Well, let's load up," the Lieutenant says. "It's been a long day."

"It's not over yet," I add, looking forward to a little Q & A session with Bandar.

A plan is already forming in my head.

Bandar sits in the ever-popular white plastic chair in the interrogation room. Mike and Biggie sit beside me. Outside, it is the quiet calm before dawn. I hold two cell phones in my lap, one blue and one black. I lift them up for Bandar to see. He has a receding hairline and dark brown eyes. Biggie translates.

"Which of these phones belongs to you?" I ask.

"The blue one," he replies.

I turn on the blue one and the screen lights up. After the phone completes its initiation, I select the address book and scroll through the names. The first name is Asad.

"Who is Asad?" I ask.

"That is my friend," Bandar answers.

I scroll to the next name. "Who is Diya?"

"That is my brother."

"Who is Farhan?"

"That is one of my customers."

"Does your sister know him?"

"No."

I scroll farther down the list. "Who is Ghazi?"

"He is another one of my customers."

"Does your sister know Ghazi?"

Bandar tilts his head.

"No," he says cautiously.

I show him the phone's screen, with more names in the address book. "So you know all the names on this list?"

"Yes," he answers.

"And this is your phone?" I ask.

Bandar leans back in his chair. He glances at Mike and then back at me and crosses his arms.

"Yes," he replies.

"Then answer me this," I say. "How can that be? Because I switched the SIM cards in these phones before I came in."

I suspected that he would lie about which phone was his so I played a little trick. Interrogators know how to adapt to deception.

Bandar sits in silence.

"How is it that you say the blue phone is your phone, but you know all the names from the SIM card that I took out of the black phone, including your customers?"

Bandar shuts his eyes and hangs his head.

"So you start with a lie," I say, "but I'm willing to forgive it, even though that is no way to treat your hosts. I've treated you with respect."

He looks up.

"It's okay," I say. "I expected that you would lie because you are scared."

"I am not involved," he says.

"I'm just letting you know that there is no reason to be afraid. We are not after you."

Bandar uncrosses his arms and places his hands on his legs—a sign that he might be breaking.

"We want to work with you. We are not after you or your brother-in-law, but we need to talk to him."

Bandar throws his hands up in the air.

"I do not know where is Nasim! I swear to Allah!"

"Okay, okay," I say. "Calm down. No need to get excited."

Bandar places his hands on his legs and rubs them.

"Who is Nasim's best friend?"

"His business partner, Mahmoud."

"Do you know where Mahmoud lives?"

"No. I've only met him once."

"When was that?"

"One week ago he came to the house. He wanted to stay with us but Nasim told him no. Then they left together. That night, Nasim called to say that he was not coming home for a while."

"Did he say why not?"

"No."

"Do you know Mahmoud's job?"

"I think he owns trucks. I heard that he goes to Iran for business."

"Has Nasim ever had weapons in the house?"

"Never. He would not do that because of his wife and children."

"So he keeps them at the truck yard?"

It's a loaded question.

"I don't know. I've never been to the truck yard."

"C'mon," Mike says, "you've never been to the truck yard?"

"Never."

"You live within a mile of it and you work on engines

and yet you expect us to believe you've never been to your brother-in-law's truck yard?"

"Because Nasim told me I could not go there. Sometimes he'll bring things back to the house for me to work on when my business is slow, but he won't let me or anyone else in the family go to the truck yard."

"What do you think is going on there that it is so dangerous?" I ask.

"I don't know," Bandar answers.

"You can't be that ignorant," Mike says. "You are a smart man if you can take apart and put back together engines."

We are working him with the Pride and Ego Up approach combined with the Fear Down approach from the Army Field Manual. We make him feel important, upping his ego, and try to alleviate his fears simultaneously. We want to him to relax while reinforcing that he has the ability to help us. At the same time, I played the trick with the phones to make him feel guilty about lying and to feel indebted to me. Now I will give him a way to make it up.

"Engine work is not that difficult," Bandar counters. "I learned it from my father."

"He must have also been a smart man," Mike says.

"Yes."

"How long has your sister been married to Nasim?" I ask.

"Twenty years."

"They have two children, right?"

"Yes, that's correct."

"Are you married?"

"Yes, my wife was there."

It dawns on me that Mariam's cousin, the twenty-something girl on the balcony with the toddler in her lap, is the fifty-year-old Bandar's wife.

"Do you have any children?"

"No, not yet. We've only been married for a year."

"Look," Mike says, "we don't want to keep you away from your wife. We know that you are not involved, but we need to talk to Nasim. Can you help us find him? Then we'll let you go and after we talk to him we'll let him go, and then all of you can go back to your lives. We have no fight with Iraqis."

"Who are you looking for?"

It's a dangerous question. We don't know what Bandar does or doesn't know and we don't want to fill him in on our knowledge gaps in case we release him, but at the same time you have to give a little to get a little. Interrogations are about taking educated risks.

"The Syrian," I say.

"Mahmoud."

"So you know he is a foreigner?"

"Yes, of course."

Biggie never interrupts an interrogation, but he sees an opportunity to help.

"The foreigners are causing trouble in Iraq," he says.
Bandar inspects Biggie's face.

"You are Iraqi?" Bandar asks.

"Yes."

"Where are you from?"

"Basra," Biggie answers.

Bandar nods. He's figured out that Biggie is Shi'a. The dynamics just became more complex. If Bandar is involved in the insurgency or with al Qaeda, he will resent Biggie, a Shi'a collaborating with Americans. Even if he's not in the insurgency, as a Sunni he might hold grudges against Shi'a. On the other hand, it's possible that he has friends that are Shi'a or that his family is intermarried, which is quite common, in which case he might be sympathetic. Circles within circles within circles.

"Foreigners have their hands in everything in Iraq," Bandar answers.

His innuendo is not lost on us. He is referencing the influence of Iran on Iraq's new Shi'a-dominated government. Or, perhaps, he's referring to us—Americans.

"We are a lot like you," Mike says. "We don't want to be here any more than you do. We want to go home to our families, but our government sent us here to find the foreigners that are causing all the violence in Iraq and they won't let us go home until we find them. We can work together to do that. Sunnis and Americans together. After we get rid of the foreigners, then we can go home."

"What happens to us Sunnis after you leave?" he asks.

"Then all Iraqis can work together," Biggie says.

Bandar crosses his arms again. "I don't think that is possible. There is too much history."

Our interrogation stalls. We try for four more hours to convince Bandar to tell us where to find Nasim or Mahmoud, but he claims no knowledge of their whereabouts. We need a new strategy. It's not uncommon to try an approach and fall flat on your face. The trick is to innovate, leverage your intellect, adapt to the environment, and persist. That's what we plan to do—after a quick lunch and shower. There's no sleep in our future.

After a quick shower, we take the SUV to the chow hall. We sit down with our trays of food at a long table, listening to the rock 'n' roll band.

"Halliburton rocks," I say.

"I wonder if the Albanians appreciate this dose of American culture?" Mike replies.

He bites into grilled chicken on a French baguette. I stick my fork into a plate of rigatoni.

"What do you think about Bandar?" I ask.

"It's hard to tell if he's lying or just doesn't like Americans," Mike replies.

"Or Shi'a," I say.

"He didn't appear to have any love lost for Biggie."

I take another bite of pasta.

"Any word on our return date?" Mike asks.

We've been gone from home for a total of seven months counting our training. I've reached out to our headquarters about our return date but received no reply. When the air force lends people to the army, one is always concerned that the agreed-upon six months could stretch into the army standard of a year, or more. The task force we support rotates units much quicker, yet interrogators run at their pace for the entire time we are attached. As a single guy, I have no complaints other than the waves I'm missing. Mike, however, has a family anxiously waiting back home.

"I'll continue to bug them," I say, "with an e-mail or a call every day until they answer."

It's not just Mike that I'm worried about. There are three additional air force agents who deployed with us back at the main prison. One of them is moving the week after his return, another has a date for a training course that can't be missed, and the last is a reservist and has a civilian job that he has to get back to. All of them have families.

Our air force command's contribution to the war has been significant. We've lost six agents and had several others seriously injured. We've supported several combat missions where the army has fallen short of people and our performance has been complimented by commanders across both theaters. We bring with us not only investigative skills, highly desirable for conducting counterinsurgency, but also experience in foreign liaison.

Shortly after 9/11, I spent three years conducting liaison across Latin America performing counterintelligence missions and criminal investigations. I spent another year in Korea doing the same and deployed at the beginning of the Iraq war to Saudi Arabia, where I commanded a unit of special agents that protected our largest airbase from terrorist attacks. My experience, like that of many of my fellow agents, covers work in more than thirty countries, and our relationship-building skills and knowledge of cultures are invaluable assets in the interrogation room and out in the field. In addition, our criminal investigations training taught us to see every suspect as an individual with unique motivations. Those credentials are part of the reason we have been so successful. But those skills are also liabilities when it comes to going home. If the task force had its way, we would stay forever.

We finish our meals and return to the office.

"What approach do you want to try?" Mike asks.

"We've tried Pride and Ego Up with Fear Down. We've also mixed in Love of Family and even a little bit of Futility. We could go with Establish Your Identity."

"Ah, accuse him of being a bigger fish," Mike answers.

"What do you think?" I ask.

"He's pretty sure of himself. He might find that a challenge."

"We could accuse him of being Nasim's boss and the leader of the cell."

"My concern is that he knows we are planning right now and he'll see through it," Mike says.

One disadvantage of rotating through approaches is that it can become obvious that you are struggling. That's why it's so important to spend plenty of time on the front end, analyzing motivations. It increases the probability that you will start off with the right approach.

"We need to return to square one," I say. "What makes him tick?"

"Not sure," Mike says.

"If he is a mechanic in his brother-in-law's garage, it could be money."

"Or it could be family obligations."

"Or, maybe, working for Nasim is his way of paying a dowry."

"Ah . . ." Mike says. "You might be on to something."

"But how would we approach him, then?" I ask.

"Offer him a chance to get out from under his obligation to Nasim?"

"He might not want to get out of the obligation."

"What if there was a way for him to repay the entire obligation and then some?" Mike asks.

"What if we gave him the opportunity to put Nasim in a position to make more money?"

204

"I know where you are going with this," Mike says.

"We tell him that Nasim has been selected to work with us against al Qaeda and that it involves a lot of money."

"To prepare for the upcoming war with Iran," Mike adds. "Since we've already asked him about Iran, it makes sense."

"Enlist him in a conspiracy," I say.

The conspiracy approach is a twist on two approaches in the Army Field Manual—the Incentive Approach and the Pride and Ego Up. There's an incentive for the detainee to assist Sunnis in their conflict with the Shi'a and to possibly get out of prison or receive a reduced sentence. This approach also strokes a detainee's pride, emphasizing their importance as a key player in a future conflict with Iran. Finally, it is tailored for the culture—there is a long history of tribal conspiracies. My one regret about using this approach is that it is a half promise. A future court will look favorably on a detainee who cooperates, so there is a real carrot at the end of the stick, but we have no formal program for working with Sunnis. We should.

When I was overseeing criminal investigations, we routinely ran dirty sources. Prosecutors cut deals with drug dealers and gang leaders to work up the ladder. Because al Qaeda is organized and operates like a criminal organization and not like rank-and-file soldiers, running dirty sources is a great tactic to use against them. There is a divide between Sunni and Shi'a and also between Iraqis and foreigners that is ripe for leveraging into alliances. The large majority of Sunni Iraqis are moderate Muslims and they are proud of their Iraqi heritage. They resent foreigners who treat them as inferior and al Qaeda has consistently put foreigners in positions of power in Iraq. Exploiting this fact was partially how my team convinced an Iraqi spiritual advisor in al Qaeda's inner circle to sell out Zarqawi.

In the case of Bandar, we need to figure out what motivates him. It's time to pull out the psychological scalpel.

Bandar sits with his arms crossed.

"When can I go home?" he asks.

Tiny translates.

"Soon, my friend," I answer. "First, tell me about your life."

"My life?"

"Yes, where are you from?"

"I was born in Kirkuk."

"Do you have family in Kirkuk?"

"Yes, my parents, brothers, sisters, cousins, nephews, nieces—all of them live here."

"Have you ever traveled outside Kirkuk?" Mike asks.

"Never."

"Would you like to go outside Kirkuk?"

"I want to make the Hajj once in my life."

The Hajj, or pilgrimage to Mecca, is one of the five pillars of Islam.

"Would you go alone?" I ask.

"No, I would like to take my wife and brothers."

"You know, I have a friend in Saudi Arabia."

"Who?"

"He is a general in the army," I exaggerate.

The guy I know is a colonel and lives in a Bedouin tent in the desert.

"He's a member of the royal family," I continue. "We talk all the time."

Bandar uncrosses his arms. "How did you meet him?"

"I met him when I was working in Saudi Arabia a few years ago. He owns a home in Mecca. I remember the picture he showed me. What a house! Or should I say palace?"

I stare into imaginary space, creating in my mind the nonexistent home.

"Sounds big," Mike says.

"What if . . . ." I say. "What if . . . no . . . well . . . maybe."

"What?" Bandar asks.

"I wonder if I could make a call . . . if the border between Iraq and Saudi Arabia is open."

Bandar scoots to the edge of his chair. We came into the interrogation booth with a plan—to appeal to Bandar's ego and enlist him in a conspiracy. In a matter of minutes, all of that has gone out the window. An interrogator's strength is flexibility. I'm back to an incentive approach.

"Would you go to Saudi Arabia if I could arrange it?" I ask.

Bandar scratches at his chin, inspecting me. He glances at Mike and then at me again.

"I can bring my wife?" he asks.

His wife is starting to take a much larger role than either of us expected.

"Of course," Mike says.

"Would you like to bring one of your brothers also?" I ask.

Bandar nods his head.

My mind is racing. Can it be done? A phone call to the embassy in Baghdad? Would they do it for an opportunity to find Mahmoud? It's improbable. The bureaucracy alone is overwhelming, especially getting the Saudis on board. I doubt they would allow an Iraqi with possible ties to al Qaeda into their country.

"Let me think about it," I say. "Maybe I'll make a phone call."

"*Shukran,*" Bandar replies.

"You must really care for your wife," Mike says.

"She is the light of my life," Bandar replies.

It's a lesson we learn over and over again in Iraq: the strength of romantic love, even in the most hardened members of al Qaeda. They have wives and fiancées and lovers. We cannot afford to stereotype our enemies as men who have sworn off everyone in their lives to carry out violence. Regardless of their crimes or acts of terror—however horrendous—they still love. Sometimes that love extends to combat.

Westerners think that we are the only ones who are permitted a romantic vision of war. Muslims share the same romantic notion within their culture. I call it the Lore of the Holy Warrior. The mujahideen who fought against the Soviets in Afghanistan returned as legendary heroes. They were the descendants of the holy warriors who fought against the Crusaders.

Some politicians and military leaders in our government see this war as a religious war against these holy warriors, but Iraq contradicts this oversimplified view. Al Qaeda is a tiny, fringe element of Islam. The extremists are in a marriage of convenience with other Muslims who bear grievances against us. We will have to eliminate, sometimes through force, the extremists when they threaten us, but we should never write off the chance that we can convince even the most hardened members of al Qaeda to cooperate. It's a challenge that every interrogator enjoys.

The interrogator's job is not to perpetuate stereotypes. His job is to establish common ground in order to convince a detainee to cooperate. It takes skill, cunning, cultural knowledge, and "the gift of gab"—'gator lingo that refers to a great conversationalist. Everyone knows someone with the gift of gab. It's that person who can talk to anyone and grab their interest. It's the most important trait in an interrogator, alongside empathy and cultural acumen.

Interrogations are science and art, although the science has never been fully developed in this career field. Most of our conclusions about interrogation methods are based on the actual experiences of interrogators. Still, at the end of the day, an interrogation boils down to those last few seconds where you make your pitch and hope the detainee bites. You can't afford to stumble.

"What if we could make your wife's face light up like the sun?" I ask. "Imagine the look on her face if you come home and tell her that you are going to take her to Mecca."

A smile emerges on Bandar's face. Tiny reinforces it with one of his own.

"Let's work together," Mike says.

"Yes, let's help each other out," I add.

The smile fades from Bandar's face and he crosses his arms again. Then he turns to Tiny and rattles off a story as Mike and I wait. When Bandar finishes he sits with his arms folded while Tiny explains.

"He says that Americans killed his first son. Apparently there was some type of gunfight a year ago and his son was shot and killed, accidentally. He says that he doesn't blame us because it was an accident. He claims that he is not angry about it, but his wife will never accept our help."

Hearts and minds. Winning at counterinsurgency always comes back to hearts and minds. Bandar may bear no malice toward Americans after the accidental death of his son, but it still hinders us. Collateral damage has a cost.

"I'm sorry about your son," Mike says.

"You must forgive us," I add. "I'm sure it was not intentional."

Bandar replies with a wave of the hand.

"The past is the past," he says.

"But this is an opportunity for us to make things better," Mike says.

"Yes," I add, "we can show your wife that we are sorry."

"I wish," Bandar says, "but her heart is locked and she's thrown away the key."

In some interrogations, you do everything right, but the odds are stacked against you. We've reached an impasse. It's like a game of poker where all the cards are never revealed. Bandar could be lying. Perhaps he never had a son. We need to reassess our strategy.

"I'm sorry," I say. "I wish there was a way we could work together. Unfortunately, you'll still have to go to Abu Ghraib."

"But I cannot help you!" he replies.

"Nothing I can do," I say, looking to Tiny and Mike. "Rules are rules. Shall we take a break?"

"Good idea," Mike says.

I motion to Bandar to stand and put his hands behind his back so that I can handcuff him. Mike heads for the door and as he turns the knob, Bandar speaks:

"I can't help you, but maybe someone else can."

Mike turns. "Who?"

"Nasim has a friend that drives trucks to Iran. His name is Hamza."

"Okay, go on," I say.

"I know where he lives," Bandar says.

Suddenly, I realize that Bandar must be a member of Nasim's al Qaeda cell. If he's willing to hand us Hamza, it's because he knows that we already have him.

"No deal," I say. "You're handing us fish we've already caught and you know it."

I pull him toward the door.

"Wait," Bandar says, holding his ground. "There is someone else."

"You're wasting our time," Mike says.

"I'm sick of the lies," I add. "We treat you with respect and all we get in return is lies."

I pull on his arm.

"Walid," he says.

I stop.

"I thought Nasim used the name Walid," I say.

"No," Bandar says. "Walid is Nasim's other business partner."

Hamza must have lied. He was trying to cover for Walid by saying that he and Nasim were one and the same.

"Where does Walid live?" Mike asks.

"I don't know," Bandar replies.

"Let's go," I say and pull him a step farther.

"No, wait!" he pleads.

I stop again.

"His address is in my phone."

"We already have his address," I say.

Walid's address was on the list taken from Abu Azir, but the spooks confirmed that it was a vacant house.

"Besides, you are lying," I say. "I didn't see Walid's name in your phone."

"It's not under the name Walid," he says. "It's Ghazi."

Another address for Walid right under our noses? I pull the phone from my pocket and select the address book. I scroll to the name Ghazi and look at the address. Mike pulls out a copy of the list from Abu Azir. Tiny assists and we compare the addresses. They aren't the same. I turn to Bandar.

"Why do you have Walid's address in your phone?"

"Because I am fixing the engine to his car. It is the one in Nasim's garage."

We drop Bandar with the guards and hurry over to the command post. It's almost midnight. Jeff is behind his desk flipping through papers. He looks up.

"Mahmoud's men just struck again," he says. "Two more beheadings last night."

"We have an address for Walid," Mike says.

Templeton overhears the conversation and rolls over in his chair.

"Walid?" Jeff asks. "Is it the same as the address on the list?"

"No," I say, "it's a new one."

I hand him a piece of paper with the coordinates of the house. Templeton looks at his watch.

"Six hours until we board," he says. "The new unit's plane just landed."

"Time for one last mission?" Jeff asks.

"Damn," Templeton says under his breath.

He looks again at his watch and counts on his fingers. This is what makes the task force so successful—they jump out of their seats to do the mission.

"The advance members from the new team are already settled in," Templeton says. "We'll take them with us. Make the call. Strykers in ten minutes."

Fire in the Oven

July 7, 2006

MAHMOUD
(A.K.A. ZAFAR)
↑
MUHAMMAD
↑
WALID
↑
NASIM
↑
BANDAR
↑
HAMZA

As we're loading into the Strykers, Jeff approaches. "Wait," he says. "This is important. We have reason to believe that Walid is connected to Muhammad, one of Mahmoud's brothers."

Jeff hands us an intel card with the latest wire diagram. There's a new link in the chain. It feels like we're going backward.

As we pull out of the parking area, I hold the hand grip above and slosh around with the bumps. The Stryker jerks forward, brakes, decelerates, and turns.

The Alabama Lieutenant isn't with us—he stayed behind to help load the unit's equipment onto the C-17. In his place is the unit's operations officer, a short, muscular Captain from Georgia with little sense of humor. He's spoken less than five sentences to us 'gators. I've seen him only a few times in the operations center, playing *Halo* on a laptop.

"Lock and load!"

We rack our rifles.

The rest of the ride is an uneventful series of starts, stops, and turns, and then the call comes for airguards. I pop the hatch and stand on the bench.

We are on a four-lane road. There are power poles along the shoulder and behind them a row of two-story homes without windows.

We turn toward the neighborhood and accelerate. I scan the rooftops through my monocle as we approach the first row of houses. The roofs are bare. We turn again onto a narrow street. Each time we turn, the TC yells at the driver to keep his distance so that we don't bunch up with the other Strykers.

There is barely a meter between my side of the Stryker and the wall that lines the street. We slow to a crawl and then come to a stop. There's a muffled call over the radio and the ramps drop. Soldiers exit and trot along the wall.

The medic grabs my pant leg and gives it a jerk. I make a last scan of the rooftops, lower myself into the Stryker, and exit out the back ramp. I follow the medic down the street, where I find the soldiers set up outside a home. Green laser beams fill the night sky. We kneel against the wall and wait. A soldier runs out the gate, turns the corner, and crouches.

"Clear," he whisper-yells.

An explosion. The soldiers race from their positions along the wall through the gate and into the house. We continue kneeling against the wall, scanning the rooftops. Five minutes pass before the Georgia Captain appears in the gateway. He slowly turns his wide-shouldered frame until he's facing us.

"You're up," he says.

Glass crunches underneath our boots as we follow the Captain into the house. We step around the metal door lying on the ground at the entrance. In the living room there are two soldiers pulling drawers out of an entertainment center and dumping the contents onto the floor.

"The raghead is out back," the Captain says. "He tried to jump the wall."

"Stay here, we'll be back," I say to Biggie and Tiny.

We pass through a cramped utility room and out the back door into a fenced yard. An Iraqi with curly black hair sits on the ground with his hands flexi-cuffed. He's wearing pajama bottoms and a white T-shirt.

"The wife and kids are in the bedroom," the Captain says.

I look at Mike. "I'll take this guy to the living room if you want to talk to the wife in the bedroom."

"Sure thing," Mike says.

I help the Iraqi to his feet, lead him into the house, and place him against a wall in the living room. He looks at the soldiers combing through his belongings. I flip up the monocle over my eye and tilt my helmet back on my head. Biggie stands next to me. His face is clearly visible in the light of the living room. He's late thirties, wild eyed, and the top of his head comes to my chin. He's a dwarf next to Biggie.

"What's your name?" I ask.

Biggie translates.

"Walid," he says.

"Walid, why did you run?"

Walid shifts his eyes to Biggie and back.

"Keep your eyes on me," I order.

He stutters his way through an answer. "I th . . . th . . . thought you were thieves."

"Are there a lot of criminals in this neighborhood?"

"No."

"Maybe you thought we were a Shi'a militia coming for you," I say.

"Maybe," Walid says.

"Why would the Shi'a be coming for you?"

"No reason."

"Who lives in this house?"

"Just me and my wife and children."

"Have you had any visitors today?"

"No."

"Are you sure?"

"I'm sure."

A glass figurine falls to the floor behind me and breaks. Walid glances at the fragments on the ground.

"What is your job?" I ask.

"I sell clothes at the market," Walid replies.

"What types of clothes?"

"Socks."

"Who works with you?"

"I work alone."

"When's the last time you left Kirkuk?"

"I haven't left Kirkuk in three years."

"Have you ever been outside of Iraq?"

"Never."

The Captain approaches, stands between me and Biggie, and stares at Walid. I have nothing so far so I decide to throw the dice. Maybe Jeff is right and he knows Mahmoud's brother.

"How do you know Muhammad?"

Walid glances at the Captain. "I don't know Muhammad."

As soon as the words leave Walid's mouth the Captain's hand comes up and grabs him by the throat. The Captain's fingers fit almost all the way around Walid's neck and he squeezes. Instantly, Walid's face turns red. I reach up and grab the Captain's wrist. I pull on it but it won't budge. He turns and glares with his other hand on his pistol. I pull again on his wrist.

"I've got this," I say.

Walid chokes. The Captain continues to glare, but I don't move. He lets go and I drop his wrist. Walid bends over and gasps for air.

"Five minutes," the Captain says and walks away.

Walid takes in several deep breaths, then stands up straight. His eyes shift rapidly. I lift my water bottle to his lips. He denies it but I insist. He takes a sip and water runs down his chin and drips onto his bare feet. I consider an apology, but decide against it.

"Look, I don't want to have to take you back to the base," I say, "because it's not you I want. I want Muhammad."

He looks up, trying to catch his breath.

"I don't want to leave your wife and kids here alone. Do you want that?"

"No," he says.

"Who's going to look after your family?"

"I don't know," he says and coughs. "But why would I help you?"

"Look, I'm sorry about—"

"All you Americans are the same," he says.

If Walid had any thoughts of cooperating, they just evaporated. The Captain successfully reinforced why Walid has picked up arms against us.

A strange odor fills the air and I recognize it as smoke. I remember that they blew the door off its hinges and it lies on the floor behind me. The smell grows stronger.

"Do you smell smoke?" I ask Biggie.

He sniffs. "Yes."

We look around the room.

"The oven!" Biggie yells.

He walks over to the stove, examines the knobs, and turns one until it clicks. He opens the oven door and smoke billows out. There's a small flame in the bottom.

"Papers!" Biggie yells.

He pulls the flaming papers out of the oven and stomps on them until they are extinguished, burning his hand in the process. He picks up the papers from the floor and places them on the counter. Some are still intact. Biggie reads through them.

"These are Ansar al-Islam pamphlets," Biggie says.

Walid grows restless on the wall.

"Got it," a soldier announces behind me.

I turn around. The cushions to the sofa are lying on the floor and the soldier has a cell phone in his hand.

"Let me see that," I say.

The soldier brings over the phone. Biggie walks over with the pamphlets and waves them in Walid's face. I select the address book on the phone and scroll through the names. The third entry is Muhammad. I place the phone in front of Walid.

"Who is this?" I ask.

He doesn't look up.

"Read the name!" I order.

Walid looks at the phone and mutters the name. "Muhammad."

"I thought you said you didn't know Muhammad."

Silence.

"Here I am trying to help you and you lied to me."

Walid doesn't move.

"You choked me!" he says.

"I stopped it," I say.

"All you Americans are the same."

"No, we're not. But now you have to decide. Either you tell me where I can find Muhammad, or I take you back to the base."

Walid looks down at his feet. I point toward the charred papers in Biggie's hands.

"What do you think is going to happen when you go to the court and they see these?"

More silence. I put my hand on his shoulder and give a light squeeze.

"My friend," I say, "I can make these papers go away. I can put them back in the oven. All you have to do is tell me where to find Muhammad."

More silence.

Mike enters the room with Walid's wife. She wears a blue cotton dress that covers her from neck to wrist to ankle, and a matching head scarf. Her eyes are lined with dark circles.

"Up here," Mike instructs her.

Walid's wife slowly comes forward, her eyes avoiding her husband. She stops a few feet away.

"Let's go through this again," Mike says. "Did you have any visitors today?"

She hesitates and Tiny repeats the question a second time in Arabic.

"Yes," she says.

"And what was the name of the visitor we talked about?"

She raises a hand to the side of her face.

"Say the name you told me," Mike says.

"Muhammad," she mumbles.

Walid continues to stare at his feet. His wife starts pleading in Arabic. It starts with soft questions but then her voice grows. Soon she is wailing and throwing her hands in the air. A tempest is raging.

"What's she saying?" I ask Tiny.

"She's telling him to think of their children," Tiny replies.

The Captain enters the room and stands behind us watching the scene. Walid doesn't look at his wife. Her voice reaches a climax. She's admonishing. Everything he's ever done wrong in their marriage is now spilling out.

A tear escapes down Walid's cheek. His head twitches. The Captain clears his throat.

Walid looks up at his wife and she stops in midsentence. The room falls quiet. Walid speaks to her in Arabic. She replies. He shuffles on his feet and then his wife says something that needs no translation. *Please.*

Walid looks up at me, pauses, and speaks. "Muhammad lives far from here. I can tell you how to get there but I don't want to go."

The Captain looks at his watch and curses.

Walid's wife turns and walks to the bedroom, wiping her tears on her sleeve and mumbling under her breath. She's complaining about men.

The guards place Walid in a cell as we return to our office and remove our gear. There's a helicopter on the way to take Walid to the main prison. They want him quickly because of his connections to Iran.

"Who would have thought he would cave to his wife?" I ask.

"Just another thing Iraqis and Americans have in common," Mike replies.

"I already gave the coordinates to Jeff," I say.

"I wonder how long until we launch on Muhammad's house."

"We probably have just long enough to take a shower and put on clean uniforms. Or eat," I say.

We have a long running joke about the proper timing of showers. Several times we'd just put on fresh uniforms when the Bat Phone rang. Every day we have to choose between showers and chow.

"I'm going to take my chances on the shower," Mike says, "if only for the feeling of being clean for five minutes."

"Okay," I agree.

As we step out into the morning light, we hear the roar of a cargo plane and turn to see a C-17 lifting off. Major Templeton scored a last-second goal. We captured Walid. In my short three and a half weeks with the team we've captured four major al Qaeda members: Omar, Abu Azir, Hamza, and Walid. Bandar was transferred to the main prison and might prove to be the fifth. Four of the five men were captured as a result of information obtained through interrogations. The army's secret weapon in this war isn't technology. It's the American brain.

After our showers, we return to the office and turn on the television. The World Cup Final is just starting. France and Italy face off in a classic showdown—the perennial powerhouse Italians versus the 1998 champions. Both teams score once in the first twenty minutes, but then go scoreless for the rest of regular time. In extra time neither team scores but the French star, Zinedine Zidane, is sent off for head-butting an Italian player. The game has to be decided by penalty kicks. I pray the Bat Phone doesn't ring.

The French miss their second attempt, but the Italians make five out of five shots and win their first World Cup in twenty-four years.

"You called it," Mike says.

"A game for the record books," I reply.

"What should we watch now?" Mike asks.

"How about—"

The Bat Phone interrupts.

13

The Eagle and the Chickens

July 9, 2006

Sometimes targets of opportunity arise that are so juicy and tempting, you can't resist. The civil war in Iraq started a month before my arrival with the February bombing of the Golden Dome Mosque, also known as the al Askariya Shrine, one of the holiest sites for Shi'a Muslims and the final burial place for two adored ninth-century imams. It is also the location where many Shi'a believe the mysterious twelfth imam will return during the apocalypse to cleanse the world of infidels.

Zarqawi claimed responsibility for the attack and no one doubted it, but who specifically carried out the mission is still a mystery. One name thrown around as the probable mastermind is Haitham al-Badri.

Haitham al-Badri is an al Qaeda bogeyman. He was a warrant officer in the Republican Guard under Saddam

Hussein and after Saddam's fall, he joined the violent insurgent group Ansar al-Sunna. He later merged his cell
with al Qaeda and became the leader of al Qaeda in the
Salahuddin Province in northern Iraq, which includes
the city of Samarra—home to the Golden Dome Mosque.
Coalition forces have been searching for al-Badri for
years. He's another Zafar—a man who exists only in rumors. But then the task force catches a break. A tip comes
in that he is at a safehouse in the countryside outside Samarra. A strike team in central Iraq launches immediately.

Most of the strike team attacks the house. As they dis-
mount from the choppers, they're greeted by a hail of gun-
fire. A heated firefight unfolds and the strike team can't
push across the yard and into the house. The insurgents
inside are well armed and have plenty of ammunition to
feed their automatic weapons.

A standoff ensues. Should the insurgents try to run,
they'd be cut down before they could take three steps toward freedom.

But who is in the house? Why are they willing to die
when so many others simply throw up their hands and
beg, "Mister . . . Mister . . ."

Minutes before the raid, a white truck departed the
house. A second strike team inside choppers pursues it.

They catch up a few miles down the road and nab four men inside without a shot fired. Three AK-47s are recovered from inside the vehicle.

"You mean they're still shooting it out?" I ask Jeff.

He pushes his glasses back up his nose. The task force has not been in a sustained firefight since my arrival. The raids by our shooters are swift and fatal to the insurgents.

"Yeah, that's why we need to get on this right away," Jeff says. "They brought all four detainees from the truck here because the main prison is full. We need to find out what they know about the insurgents in the house as fast as possible and get it back to the strike team."

"Okay," I reply, "we'll do our best."

"Matthew . . ." Jeff says, his expression grim.

"Yeah?"

"We have casualties. At least one of our guys has been wounded."

I wake up Mike and the terps. This is going to be an all-nighter. We put the four men from the truck into separate booths. I take two and Mike takes two. We use all the tricks in our tool bag, but they claim to be farmers on their way home from selling produce at a local market. The guns in the truck, they claim, are for self-defense, since the roads are no longer safe.

It seems plausible enough, except all four deny they

ever visited the house in question. We know that's a lie and have video to prove it.

The interrogations drag on for hours. A pattern emerges. One of the detainees, Tariq, is unusually calm where the other three are a nervous wreck. Tariq radiates confidence.

Who is this guy?

Jeff calls and tells us that the strike team called in close air support. There's nothing left of the house but a smoking hole in the ground. We call it quits and decide to try again in the morning.

The rest of the evening, I ponder this new detainee, Tariq. I've seen his name before. I dig around through old reports but come up empty. I call Jeff but he also comes up with nothing. This guy is too collected and confident to be just another al Qaeda foot soldier.

July 10, 2006

I wake up early the next morning, grab Biggie, rouse the dozing guards, and put Tariq into an interrogation room, where we sit face-to-face. He looks like he just walked out of a Toni&Guy Salon, coiffed and manicured. A metrosexual insurgent.

We exchange pleasantries. I ask him background questions. He pauses for several long seconds before he replies, calculating every word.

He claims to be a humble farmer who studied engineering at Baghdad University for three years before his father died suddenly after the fall of Saddam. He won't divulge the circumstances of his father's death, which makes me suspect it was at the hands of a Shi'a militia or Americans.

After his father's death, Tariq returned home to run the family farm and take care of his mother and brothers. Having gained an understanding of why he may have joined al Qaeda, I press with less benign questions.

"What were you doing at that house yesterday?" I ask.

"Hmph," he replies with a casual shrug of the shoulders. He picks at lint on his pants and flicks it onto the floor.

"I know you were at the house, Tariq. We have you on camera."

"Wrong car," he says.

"Definitely not the wrong car," I reply. "We followed you from the house."

"Hmph," he says and picks more lint from his pants.

"Would you like to see the video?" I ask.

"You Americans can alter videos," he says. "You do it all the time."

He may be referring to a common-held belief in the

Middle East that Americans doctor videos for propaganda purposes. It's hard to refute the claim, however false. Hollywood *is* an American creation.

We go in circles and three hours later I end the interrogation. Tariq's obnoxious "hmph" echoes in my head throughout the day. My instincts tell me that Tariq is a big fish. Jeff calls and says that we'll have him another day.

Halfway through an episode of *Band of Brothers*, I have an epiphany and realize where I've seen Tariq's name. A couple months ago, we snared a couple of interesting insurgents in a raid in Salahuddin Province. One was a nineteen-year-old foreign fighter from Somalia. We have a section in our task force devoted entirely to foreign fighters and although they have their own interrogators and analysts, I was in charge of monitoring them to ensure they played by the rules.

I observed the African kid's interrogations and read the intelligence reports. He had come to Iraq to become a mujahideen and to fight against the infidels. Instead, al Qaeda told him he would be a suicide bomber, something he resisted. He wanted to fight, not detonate.

By the time we captured him, he was completely disillusioned with al Qaeda and told us everything we wanted to know, including who he thought was behind the Golden Dome Mosque bombing. He'd heard it was a man called

The Leader, who was none other than Haitham al-Badri, but his information was secondhand.

Along with the African kid the strike team brought in a scholarly looking Iraqi named Hasan. In his house, the shooters found a ledger book. Hasan, it turns out, was the bookkeeper for al-Badri's network, but he wouldn't talk. At the time of Hasan's capture, I had an interpreter translate several pages of the ledger. It contained every expense al-Badri paid to his cells during a six-month period, listing purchases, weapons allocations, and sources of income. There was a name that popped up throughout the ledger—Tariq.

I call the main prison and get them to fax a copy of the ledger. I take it to Biggie.

"What's this?" he asks as I hand him the book.

"This is Haitham al-Badri's account book."

"Really?" Biggie asks.

"Yes. Can you find a name in there for me?"

"What name?"

"Tariq."

He flips through the pages.

"Here," he says and pokes a page.

"What's it say?" I ask.

"It says: '$10,000 to Tariq for explosives.' "

Could this be the same Tariq? Could he be in al-Badri's cell?

"Here it is again," Biggie says, scanning another page. " 'Tariq replaces Rashad.' "

"Thanks, Biggie," I say.

"Look at this!" Biggie continues.

"What?"

"Says here 'payment for power lines.' What do you think that means?"

"Let's ask him." I head back to the office to think.

What serendipity this would be if the guy in our cell is the Tariq in the ledger. First, I have to get him to talk. He won't move off his "farmer on the way home from the market" story. Could he be innocent?

No. He was at the house. We have him on film. Why is he sticking to a story that can't possibly hold water?

Maybe he understands interrogation techniques and stays with the story to defeat my approaches. So far, it has worked. My respect for Tariq goes up a notch.

What motivates him? What are his weaknesses?

In every interrogation he was composed, bordering on arrogance, as if he were above the whole process.

Arrogance. What causes him to be arrogant in these dire circumstances? Perhaps he's a leader. He's used to giving orders and commanding respect.

Ego. Confidence. Charisma. There's a way to exploit these traits.

The other three men are uneducated. Their hands are calloused. Perhaps they are Iraqi farmers turned insurgents. But not Tariq.

Mike enters the office and decides to take another crack at one of Tariq's comrades. He departs and I'm left alone with my thoughts.

Band of Brothers ends. The men of Easy Company parachuted behind the German defenses at Normandy. The element of surprise takes the Germans off guard and the Allies capture their objective. The element of surprise.

Tariq is the Germans at Normandy. He's entrenched in his story. Why confront him head on? Why not parachute in behind enemy lines?

I hurry to Mike's interrogation booth. A quiet knock and Mike opens the door and joins me in the hallway.

"Hey, do you think you can get your guy to write a statement saying that Tariq was not responsible for their capture?"

Mike raises his eyebrows. "What are you up to?"

"Let's just say inspiration struck."

"Okay," Mike says. "Give me a minute."

The door closes and I wait. Minutes later Mike opens the door and hands me a piece of paper.

"Thanks," I say.

"Tell me about it later, okay?"

"Sure thing."

I go to the terp den, grab Biggie, and ask him to

translate the sentence on the piece of paper. "It says that Tariq is not responsible for their capture."

"Okay, how do I rewrite it to say that Tariq *is* responsible?"

"Just remove this word," Biggie points.

Together we trace a new copy, leaving out the Arabic that translates to "not." When we're done, it looks perfect. The handwriting is identical, except now it is an accusation, not an absolution.

Tariq sits casually in the plastic chair, picking lint off his pants.

"I have some good news and some bad news," I say.

"Hmph," Tariq says.

"The good news is that you are about to be released."

Tariq can't conceal his surprise. His self-assured poker face slips.

Usually this is a terrible tactic. Telling a prisoner he's about to get released is a surefire way to get him to clam up so he doesn't blow his chance at freedom, but I've got another card up my sleeve.

"When will I be released?" he asks.

"Soon. But you need to know something first."

"What?"

"Well . . . uhm . . ." I fumble over my words.

Tariq perks up.

You've got to sell this, I tell myself.

"Tariq," I say, "your comrades are pretty angry with you."

His eyes widen. "They are angry with me? Why? Did you tell them I gave you information?"

"Oh no," I say. "They are angry because they blame you for getting captured. We can't give back the guns— that's one of the rules. Your friends are saying that you'll have to pay off the money that they've lost."

"Hmph," Tariq says.

His face flushes scarlet and he utters an Arabic curse under his breath. I continue the charade.

"They said that if you hadn't forgot your weapon at the house and had to go back for it then they would never have been captured."

Tariq curses again in Arabic. He turns and scowls at the wall, face red with anger.

"Anyway, I thought you should know," I say.

Still frowning at the wall, he sputters unintelligible words. Then he turns to me. "These stupid farmers."

He eyeballs me with a worried expression. I act like I don't notice.

"Tariq, can I ask you something?" I ask.

"Yes," he says.

"Why are you with these guys?"

"What do you mean?"

"Well, you're an intelligent man, but they appear to be ignorant farmers."

"That's because they *are* ignorant farmers!" he replies.

"Ahhh," I say. "It must be tough being an eagle flying with chickens."

Tariq growls, "Chickens are stupid creatures!"

I smile. "Maybe . . . but these chickens can write."

I hand him the forged statement.

Tariq snatches the paper from my hand. His hands shake as he reads it. He recognizes the handwriting. By the time he's done, his face is almost purple.

"Did the others see this statement?" he demands.

"Yes," I lie.

He frowns and turns to stare at the wall. Silence. He's ready to erupt. He turns back again.

"Stupid Karim!" he says. "He is the reason why we are all here!"

"How so?"

"The idiot forgot his weapon. He told us that he knew the people at the house and he could get another one."

"How many people were there?" I ask.

"Ten."

"Iraqis?"

"No. Most were foreigners."

"How did Karim know he could get a weapon there?"

"Because his brother lives there. It is his house. And he is just as big an idiot as Karim."

I laugh. Tariq joins in. I've thrown him off his game. He's vulnerable. Time to go for the kill. I hand him Hasan's ledger book.

"What's this?" he asks.

"Is that you, mentioned?" I ask, pointing to a line with his name.

Tariq reads it. He looks up, studies my face, and then looks again to the ledger.

"Yes," he says.

There's pride in his voice.

"It says that you took over for Rashad as al Qaeda's commander in Salahuddin Province."

"That is true."

"That is a position of great respect."

"Naturally."

"Who do you work for?"

He doesn't hesitate.

"The Leader."

"Who is The Leader?" I ask.

Tariq picks a piece of lint off his pants and throws it on the floor. "I do not know his name. I met him only once on the side of a road."

"Describe him," I say.

"He is average height and weight. Dark hair and eyes."

"Is The Leader Haitham al-Badri?" I ask.

"He never told me his name."

I remove a photo of Haitham al-Badri from a file under my chair. It's a blurry image of a man in a military uniform, wearing sunglasses.

"Is this The Leader?" I ask, handing the photo to Tariq.

He inspects it. "This could be anybody. It could be me."

Could Tariq be Haitham al-Badri? I take the photo. I hold it in front of me with Tariq's face off to the side. No, it's not him.

"You are scared of Haitham," I say. "I understand that. He blew up the Golden Dome Mosque."

Tariq ignores the comment, picks another piece of lint from his pants, and flicks it onto the floor.

"What does this entry mean?" I say, pointing to a line on another page of the ledger.

Tariq reads it.

"The power lines," he says.

"Yes."

"The government pays farmers every month to lease their property where they put electrical transmission towers. We take a share of that money from the farmers for protection."

It's an old mob racket. Extortion.

"What happens if they refuse?"

Tariq offers a devilish smile. "We blow up the tower. Then the farmer loses the lease."

"That's very clever," I say.

Tariq grins.

"You know, Tariq, a man with such skills and intelligence as you possess must have met The Leader more than once."

He considers this.

"That is true," he concedes.

"Where did you meet?"

Silence.

"If you tell us where we can find The Leader, I can help you."

He smiles. "I know what's going to happen to me. And I know that you can't help me."

"Why do you say that?" I ask.

"You have the ledger. It's proof that I have killed many Americans. I will pay for that."

"Perhaps not. I might be able to get you back to your family. Didn't you say that you recently got married?"

"Yes, but I will never see her face again."

He shrugs. The turtle goes back into his shell. For another hour I try approach after approach, but I cannot puncture his fatalism. He offers up the locations of two possible al Qaeda safe houses, but doesn't lead me to Haitham al-Badri.

Interrogations are about incremental breaks. These small tidbits of information—confirmation of Haitham's nickname, a partial physical description, where he and

Tariq once met, etc.—appear insignificant, but combined with dozens of other such tidbits from various intelligence sources, paint a picture. This one small break might be the single remaining piece of the puzzle that we need to pinpoint Haitham al-Badri.

After the interrogation ends, I go to the command post and tell Jeff who we have in the cell block. It's not often that we capture an al Qaeda leader who controls an entire province, and is only one degree of separation removed from Haitham al-Badri.

Later that night, Mike takes Tariq's information into the interrogation room with the farmers. They confirm the locations of the safehouses, but give us nothing on Haitham al-Badri. They also refuse to provide information about Tariq. The fear in their voices confirms Tariq's position.

July 11, 2006

The following morning, Jeff informs us that the main prison has requested Tariq. As soon as his identity was transmitted in my intelligence report, the phone started ringing. Everyone wants a piece of him. In the hour before he leaves I interrogate Tariq one last time, but he's hunkered down inside his shell, resigned to his fate. He never gives up an exact location for Haitham al-Badri, but he does confirm information from the ledger and explains al Qaeda's grand strategy. They have given up Baghdad and Anbar Province. They are setting up operations in northern Iraq. Money, weapons, supplies, and foreign fighters are moving north. The leader in the north is a Syrian—a man who goes by the name Zafar.

The conclusion is clear. Zafar, a.k.a. Mahmoud, is working with Haitham al-Badri. If we don't find him soon, there will be another Golden Dome Mosque bombing and Iraq will be lost to all-out civil war.

14

The Generator

Every sun has to set. —ARAB PROVERB

July 12, 2006

In the predawn hours we enter the conference room, which is filled with a new crowd of tattooed soldiers. The new commander, Major Mitchell, has called the entire unit together for a briefing. Jeff sits at the front of the room, preparing the team's first intelligence briefing. Jeff and we interrogators are the unit's continuity.

Mitchell walks into the room and the First Sergeant calls the room to attention. We rise from our seats.

"As you were," Mitchell orders.

We take our seats. Mitchell has reddish-brown hair combed to the side. He walks to the front of the room and stands with his hands on his hips. "I came here with two things and I'm leaving with both—my father's last name and my integrity."

He lets that sink in. Not a soul stirs as he looks around

the room. "I trust you men to do your jobs and to do them well." He turns to Jeff. "Slides."

As Mitchell takes a seat in the front row next to me, Jeff brings up the briefing. The first slide is a wire diagram. A thin line runs from name to name—Omar is at the bottom of the slide; at the top is Mahmoud/Zafar.

Mike and I are getting short. We await word from our headquarters, but we're scheduled to leave in less than two weeks. Neither of us wants to leave without catching the man who gave us the slip.

"Tonight's target is Muhammad," Jeff says. "Other intelligence has confirmed the location of his residence."

He flips the slide and a satellite photo of the target house appears on the screen. After he finishes, a shiny Second Lieutenant straight out of West Point walks to the front of the room with a laser pointer and starts the mission brief.

"Gentlemen, tonight I'll be leading the mission. Here's the breakdown . . ."

After the briefing, we exit the conference room and walk toward our office. The sun is breaking the horizon and there's a light breeze. Mitchell catches up to us.

"Gentlemen, do you have a minute?" he asks.

We turn around.

"Sure," I say.

"Templeton said that you guys are good," Mitchell says. "He told me he trusts you more than any other source of intelligence."

"We've learned a few tricks," I say.

"Keep up the good work. I want you to know that you have my full confidence. We've got a couple of young lieutenants on this rotation, but they're sharp."

"No problem," I say. "I'll keep an eye on them."

My rank has never been discussed. I'm just another 'gator, even when I was the senior interrogator at the main prison—a position based on competence, not rank. It's been enjoyable to be one of the troops for the past several months, but you can't take the feeling of responsibility out of an officer. It's ingrained in us by our training.

"I look forward to working together," Mitchell says.

"Same here," Mike replies.

Back at the office, we put on our gear. I load my SIG Sauer with a magazine while Mike clips the sling for his M-4 onto his vest.

" 'My father's last name and my integrity,' " I say. "I like this guy."

"Seems like a real straight shooter," Mike replies.

"Let's grab him a prize."

We fasten the last of our straps and head for the door.

As usual, the inside of the Stryker is a furnace. The ramp opens and we exit. Sweat runs down my legs and collects in the bottom of my boots. My feet slosh in puddles as I run down the street.

We approach the target house, and a soldier waves me in through the gate while another scans the rooftops with his rifle at the ready. In the courtyard two men lie facedown in the grass with their hands tied behind their backs. A soldier stands over them. The Second Lieutenant, his baby face flush red, strolls out the front door with half a dozen soldiers in trail. Above, a soldier on the balcony motions with his arm to the next house.

"A squirter went over the wall," the Lieutenant says as he passes. "We're going to the next house."

We take a knee in the courtyard next to a stone fountain. In this heat, the sound of falling water is torture.

"Looks like a block party," Mike says.

"Everyone's invited," I reply.

From the courtyard next door there's an explosion. A woman screams. A soldier appears on the balcony and then disappears back inside.

Next to us, the soldier standing over the Iraqi men

puts his hand to his earpiece and looks over. "They want you in the next house."

I lead the group out the gate, down the sidewalk, and turn into the next courtyard. There are two more men in restraints lying facedown in the grass; another soldier stands over them.

"Wait here, I'll find the Lieutenant," I say to Mike.

Inside the foyer I step over the metal door and into the living room. The Lieutenant is standing in the middle of the room. He takes deep breaths while he listens to the transmission in his earpiece.

"Got it!" he says, taking note of me. "I want two through five on me now! Six through eight stay here! Move it!"

"Block party?" I ask.

"We've got more squirters," he says.

Three soldiers charge down the stairs. Their green uniforms are soaked through, but they breathe easy. They line up behind the Lieutenant, swinging their muzzles deliberately toward the ground.

"We got everyone?" the Lieutenant asks.

"Check," says the last soldier in line.

"See you later," the Lieutenant says to me. He runs out the door with the soldiers in trail.

In the courtyard Mike and the terps are on a knee sipping water.

"What's up?" Mike asks.

"Definite block party," I say.

I take a knee next to them and sip from my Camel-Bak. My shoulders ache from the weight of my body armor and loaded vest. I swing my rifle to one side and rest it on the ground next to me. One of the Iraqis in the courtyard rolls to his side to alleviate the discomfort in his shoulders.

There's another explosion, another scream. A soldier appears on the roof of the next house and looks down through the scope of his rifle. We remain kneeling. More glass breaks in the distance, more yelling. Fifteen minutes pass. I consider moving the group inside where we can sit in the shade. The earpiece of the soldier standing over the Iraqis crackles.

"They want you down the street," he says. "Open gate on the left."

"You stay here with Tiny," I say to Mike. "I'll take Biggie."

Biggie and I run out the gate and down the sidewalk. We trot along a wall and then cross the street toward an open gate. There's no soldier to wave us through but I figure they're low on numbers. I step through the gate and into the courtyard. There's a blue sedan parked in the carport. The front door to the house is closed and intact. An Iraqi in a white dishdasha pops up from behind the car with something metal in his hand. I instantly raise my rifle, set my sights on him, and press my finger to the trigger. He looks at me, his eyes grow large, and he drops the wrench in his hand.

A soldier yells as he passes through the front gate into the courtyard, "Get down! Get the fuck down!"

The Iraqi raises his hands in the air. The soldier approaches him with his rifle carefully aimed.

"Down!" the soldier yells, and motions the Iraqi to the ground with his rifle.

The Iraqi quickly falls to his knees and then lies facedown on the ground next to the car with his arms straight out in front of him. Two more soldiers pass through the gate and run to the front door of the house. The first soldier kicks the door down, steps back, scans the inside of the home with his rifle, and then races inside with his partner behind him. The Lieutenant enters the courtyard from the street. His shoulders are heaving.

"Looks like you beat us here," he says.

I nod.

"This is the last house," he says. "I got no more bodies."

A soldier appears on the balcony above, looks down, and then disappears back inside.

"Let's move all the captures back to the courtyard at the first house," the Lieutenant says.

"I'll take this guy," I reply, "and meet you there."

I relieve the soldier as he finishes securing the Iraqi's hands behind his back. I help the Iraqi to his feet. We march out of the gate and back down the street to the first house. I consider what might have been.

In the courtyard there are now eight men in restraints, sitting next to each other on the grass. Their wives, sons, daughters, mothers, and sisters sit on the other side of the courtyard, cradling infants. A soldier stands in front of each group, reminding them not to talk. Mike and I stand in the middle of the courtyard between the two sides, waiting for the Lieutenant.

"What's the name of the guy we're looking for?" Biggie asks.

"Muhammad," I reply.

"It's damn hot," Mike says.

"I'm going to get them some water," I say.

I walk out the gate and into the street. A Stryker is parked in front of the house and the TC poking out the top of the vehicle nods at me.

"Mind throwing down a case of water?" I ask.

"Sure," the TC says. He pulls a box out from under the straps and pushes it over the edge. I catch it and return to the courtyard. I open the box and we distribute the water to the women and children. The women thank us, open the bottles, and allow the children to drink first. Biggie takes a bottle to the men and pours water into each of their mouths. Everyone is soaked to the bone in sweat.

The Lieutenant enters the courtyard and approaches me.

"Can't be sure we got all the squirters," he says.

"No problem," I say. "We'll work with what we have."

"Alright," he says, "try to make it quick."

Mike and I each pick one of the adult males from the first target house and lead them inside to separate rooms. I place my guy on the couch in the living room and sit next to him. Biggie pulls up a cushioned chair. It's a large room with a marble floor and an expensive glass coffee table on a red oriental rug. In the corner of the room is a black piano, over which an oil painting of the family hangs on the wall, next to a glass display case with shelves of crystal. I take off my helmet and wipe my brow on the back of my glove. My rifle hangs at my side.

The Iraqi has long black hair and a black mustache that covers his mouth. He wears khaki slacks, a crisp short-sleeve button-up, and thin black framed glasses. He sits upright.

I analyze his face. He's already prepared his answers.

"What is your name?" I ask.

"Jamal," he answers in perfect English with a slight British accent.

No dice.

"Who lives in this house?"

"My wife, my children, and my brother and his family," he replies.

"What is your brother's name?"

"Fareed."

Still no dice.

"What is your job?"

"I'm an optometrist."

He wears expensive frames.

"How long has your brother and his family been staying here?" I ask.

"Two months," he replies.

"Why are they living here?"

"Because my brother lost his job in Baghdad."

"What was his job?"

"He worked for the government."

"What did he do exactly?"

"He worked for the Department of Transportation as a civil engineer."

"How long have you been an optometrist?" I ask.

He rolls his shoulders to relieve the discomfort of his hands tied behind his back. "Twenty years."

"Where did you study medicine?" I ask.

"In London," Jamal replies.

"How long did you live there?"

"Seven years."

"When was the last time you were in England?"

"Ten years ago. One of my brothers still lives there."

"How many brothers do you have?"

"Three."

"What are their names?"

"Fadil, Latif, and Mustafa."

No Muhammad.

"Sisters?"

"Two."

"Were you ever in the military?"

"No, never."

"What about your brothers?"

"Two of my brothers were in the army. One died in the war with Iran and the other one lost a leg. He's retired and lives in Baghdad."

I search his face. The sweat on his brow is from the heat.

"I'm concerned about my family," he says.

"I gave them water and they are in the shade," I reply. "No need to worry about them."

Jamal nods and looks at Biggie. Biggie turns away and looks around the room.

"What are the names of your neighbors?" I ask.

We run through the names of his neighbors but there's no Muhammad. I try another method. "Is there an Abu Bakr on this street?"

"No."

"What about Abu Yusif?"

"No."

I hide my target within made-up names.

"Wasim?"

"No."

"Muhammad?"

"No."

"Abu Khalid?"

"No."

I decide this is going nowhere and it would be better to get a different detainee from the courtyard. We don't have a lot of time and maybe someone else will admit to knowing Muhammad.

"You have electricity," Biggie says, pointing at the air-conditioning unit mounted on the wall.

"We run a generator," Jamal says.

"A home generator?" Biggie asks.

"A diesel generator," Jamal replies. "I power the neighborhood."

"Where is the generator?" I ask.

"It's in a shed in the empty lot next to us."

Biggie raises his eyebrows.

"Let's go look at the generator," I say.

I don't know why this interests me. It's nothing more than a hunch.

I lead Jamal out of the house and into the courtyard. The Lieutenant is standing with one of his soldiers.

"There's a generator in the empty lot next door," I tell him. "I want to take a look."

He turns to the soldier standing next to him.

"Go with them," he orders.

Jamal leads us out the front gate and the soldier follows us, scanning the street and the building tops with his rifle. The empty lot is surrounded by the same stone wall that lines the street and is guarded by a gate with lock and chain. A dog barks from the other side of the gate over the hum of the generator. I look at Jamal.

"The dog is on a leash," he says. "The key to the gate is in my front pocket."

I nod to Biggie and he fishes the key out of Jamal's slacks and unlocks the gate.

"Wait," I say.

The soldier pushes open the gate door with his boot and disappears inside. A few seconds later he yells, "Clear."

The lot is a small field of brown dirt. There's a wooden shed inside and next to it is a pit bull tied by a link chain around his neck to a stake in the ground. The dog stands barking in the middle of a pool of black oil, empty plastic jugs, and refuse. Jamal utters a command in Arabic and the dog sits down in the black oil and quiets.

"In there," Jamal says, nodding toward the shed.

The soldier goes first again. The thin wooden door is unlocked and he pushes it open with his boot and clears it without stepping inside.

Jamal leads Biggie and I into the shed. The three of us barely fit inside the cramped space where the generator churns loudly. On the walls are relays, capacitors, and clumps of wires leading to rows of circuit breakers. Above each circuit breaker is a piece of tape with Arabic scribbled

on it. Biggie and I scan the breakers and then, simultaneously, turn to each other.

"Exactly," I say.

Biggie steps closer to the wall and begins to read the
names above each of the breakers. As he reads up and
down the rows, Jamal turns to look at the opposite wall
and rolls his shoulders.

"Here," Biggie says. He points to a piece of tape above
a breaker in the middle of the wall.

"Muhammad," he reads.

I turn to Jamal. He exhales.

"You said you didn't know Muhammad," I say.

Silence. I step forward and put my face close to his.
Biggie closes in with me. Jamal backs up into the cramped
corner of the shed. I lean over and put my hand on the
wall next to his head.

"You lied to me," I whisper.

He tries to back away but the wall won't allow it.

"I can forgive the lie," I say. "I understand you are
scared."

"I'm sorry . . ." he says. "I . . . I . . ."

"It's okay," I say. I put my hand on his shoulder and
give it a rub. "But please do not insult me again. I'm not
here to hurt you. I'm here for Muhammad."

"You don't understand . . . you don't . . ."

"It's okay. Tell me. What don't I understand?"

"These men . . . they are . . . dangerous."

"You let me worry about that," I say. "Where is Muhammad's house?"

Jamal rolls his shoulders, but doesn't speak.

"Do you want to work with us?" I ask. "It's not Iraqis that I'm after. I just want the foreigner."

He exhales, looks at Biggie, and then back at me.

"What will happen to my family?" he asks.

"What will happen to all the families in Iraq if we can't find a way to work together?" I ask.

Jamal closes his eyes and exhales.

"For the future of Iraq," I say, "work with me."

Jamal opens his eyes. "He was sitting next to me."

"In the courtyard?" I ask.

"Yes, in the white dishdasha."

Biggie raises his bushy eyebrows.

"Please . . . please . . . don't tell him that I told you," Jamal says. "Please . . ."

Tears roll down his cheeks from under his expensive black frames.

"My family . . . my family . . ."

Back in the courtyard, I return Jamal to the row of men sitting on the ground. The man in the white dishdasha who was previously sitting next to him is gone.

I turn and look inside the house. Mike is standing with Muhammad in the living room. I tell Biggie to wait, then walk into the house and pull Mike to the side.

"What's up?" he asks.

"Has he given you his name?"

"Yes, he said it's Hani."

"Nope. Try again."

"What do you mean?" Mike asks.

"Someone just sold him out," I reply. "That's Muhammad."

Mike turns and looks at the Iraqi. Muhammad is a squat man with a square head. He shuffles on his feet.

"How do you want to go about this?" Mike asks.

"I don't want to give up who sold him out, but we don't have a lot of time."

"Roger that," Mike says. "I have an idea."

"Go ahead."

"This guy's wife and kids are in the courtyard. All we have to do is act like we're questioning them and then come back in and say that they called him Muhammad."

"Brilliant," I say.

"I'm not done," Mike says. "I'll also tell him that they said he has a friend named Mahmoud, a Syrian that lives nearby."

"That's risky," I say. "What if Mahmoud doesn't live near here?"

"Then we're back to where we started. But if he does . . ."

An interrogator has to take risks.

"I like it," I reply.

We leave Muhammad with Tiny. Biggie joins us in the courtyard and we approach Muhammad's wife and kids.

"Do you have enough water?" I ask.

"Yes," the woman answers.

"How are your kids?" Mike asks.

"They are fine," she answers.

"How old are they?"

"Five, three, and one."

"Your husband, Muhammad, is okay," I say.

"Thank you," she answers.

Bingo.

I make small talk with Muhammad's wife while Mike returns to the house with Tiny. The Lieutenant approaches.

"How's it going?" he asks.

"We're about to find out," I say.

"Is that our target?" he asks, looking inside the house.

"Yes, but he hasn't admitted it yet. Give it a minute."

"How so?"

"An old street-cop trick," I say.

"Oh," the Lieutenant replies.

Inside the house, Mike stands in front of Muhammad and points toward his family in the courtyard. Suddenly, Muhammad drops his head. When he looks up, his lips start moving. As soon as he stops talking, Mike exits the house and approaches.

"Fifth house down on the left," Mike says.

"What?" the Lieutenant asks.

"Mahmoud is staying with his cousin. It's the fifth house down the street on the left. A blue two-story home."

Word of our block party will spread quickly and Mahmoud will move. The Lieutenant looks for soldiers and shouts orders into his mic. Instantly, soldiers appear from inside the house and line up next to him.

"Go, go, go!" the Lieutenant yells.

The soldiers race out the gate and down the street.

"Shall we?" I ask Mike.

"I'm going to stay with Muhammad," he says. "I've got a few more questions for him."

I turn to Biggie. "Let's go."

A soldier kicks in the door of the blue house and the men behind him race inside. The first floor is empty. Two soldiers climb the staircase to the second floor, rifles raised. They go room to room, but find nothing. They spot a ladder leading to the roof. One of the soldiers scales it rapidly. On the roof, he finds an empty sleeping pad and a blanket next to it. He runs to the edge of the balcony and looks down. A shadow stands against the back wall of the house.

"You!" he yells.

The shadow runs.

The soldier keys his mic.

"Squirter out the back!"

A soldier on the first floor kicks the back door open and spots the shadow running into the desert. He gives chase.

Mahmoud runs for his life, moving his short legs as fast as he can. The soldier, in full battle rattle, gains ground. Mahmoud comes within arm's reach. The soldier leaps and tackles Mahmoud in the sand. In a split second the Syrian's hands are tied behind his back.

I leave Biggie in the dust as I race for the house. Just as I arrive, a soldier is seating Mahmoud in the sand in the front yard. I recognize his small frame. I run up and drop to a knee so that we're face-to-face. He looks up. I stare into Mahmoud's blue eyes.

"Welcome back," I say.

The mysterious Zafar, a.k.a Mahmoud, the coordinator of numerous suicide bombings, a mass murderer, one of the last butchers of Iraq, is back in American hands. He sits on the floor of the Stryker at my feet. Biggie and Tiny stare at him, eyes filled with hate. This tiny man has taken thousands of lives. Innocent women and children. Grandfathers and grandmothers. Sisters, brothers, mothers, fathers, sons, and daughters. His violence didn't discriminate. And now he sits on the floor in front of me. Defenseless. Helpless. He looks up. My rifle is in my hand. Justice is within reach.

No. I will not become like you.

I don't get the chance to interrogate Mahmoud. When we arrive back at the base, a plane is already waiting to take him to the main prison. I hand Mahmoud over to the guards. Mike and I stand next to the tarmac and watch the plane taxi to the runway.

"Who would have guessed," I say, "that Muhammad would fall for such a simple trick."

"A little brain power," Mike says, "goes a long way."

An SUV pulls up. Mitchell exits and approaches.

"Gentlemen," he says. "Great job."

"One to remember," Mike replies.

"You guys are welcome on this team anytime," the major says.

The big props fill the air with red sand as the plane accelerates down the runway and takes off.

July 13, 2006

After a good six hours of sleep, Mike and I meet up at the office. The Bat Phone rings and Mike answers it. "Hello. Yes?"

He pulls the receiver to his chest.

"Strykers?" I ask.

"No, it's for you."

I grab the phone. It's Steve, an air force agent who took my place as the senior interrogator at the main prison.

"They want you back," Steve says.

"I'm sorry," I reply.

"The commander here has ordered your return. He says we're not getting enough results."

"But the plan is for Mike to return to your location. I'm to stay here and train our replacements."

"I know," Steve says, "but the commander says no questions. It's an order."

"Roger," I say and hang up the phone.

Mike's carried his fair share of risk for one tour. I'm abandoning him. Later that day, after a last trip to the rock 'n' roll chow hall and good-byes to Biggie and Tiny, I board a prop-job. As we lift off I look out the window and watch Mike, standing next to the tarmac, disappear.

July 14, 2006

Back at the main prison I return to the grind of three interrogations and fourteen hours of work per day. My partner is a new interrogator who just arrived from Guantanamo Bay. John is a likable navy guy with a positive attitude. During the first interrogation I raise my voice in frustration, asking my detainee why he won't allow me to help him. Afterward, John asks me a question in private.

"You can yell at detainees here?"

"Yes. Why?"

"At Gitmo, we can't yell anymore."

The pendulum has gone full swing. John explains that interrogators at Guantanamo have to sit behind a table, can't handle the Quran, and must have every interrogation approach approved before it is used—even the approaches in the Army Field Manual. It's micro-micromanagement. They've gone from torturing and abusing prisoners using Enhanced Interrogation Techniques to not even being able to raise their voices.

I visit Steve in the Hollywood Room, where he monitors interrogations.

"How's it going?" I ask.

"It's just not the same since you left," he says. "Don't tell anyone, but there's an order coming down today that we have to shave our beards."

"*What?*" I ask.

"Yup, that's the order. They want us to be more professional."

"What does that have to do with a beard?"

"I know," Steve says. "It helps build rapport and shows

that we respect the culture of our detainees, but that's the order."

"Did anyone argue?" I ask.

"Some people spoke up, but the First Sergeant said that our female interrogators don't have beards and they are able to interrogate."

"Uhm . . . that's because Iraqi females don't have beards," I answer.

It's another sign of the pervasive ignorance about interrogations. There are no officer interrogators in the Army. I am the highest ranking interrogator in the unit— perhaps in the entire theater—but my rank doesn't count. There are three critical sources of intelligence in this war: signal, human, and interrogations. There are officers in both the signal and human intelligence fields, but there are no officer interrogators in the army. There is no voice to argue against the madness.

"Morale is at an all-time low," Steve says.

"The best thing we can do is concentrate on interrogations," I say. "Regardless of beard shaving, we still have a job to do."

"Roger that," he says. "Any news on us going home?"

"Two weeks," I say.

"That gives me only a week before my move," Steve says.

"I know, but it's the best I could do. They wanted two months."

"Two *months?*"

"The army has a serious shortage of interrogators. They want us to overlap with our replacements. I worked out a compromise—two weeks."

"I can do that," Steve says. He gets up. "I have to go check on some reports. I'll catch up with you later."

"Sounds good," I reply.

I sit alone in the Hollywood Room watching the interrogations through the monitors. In one room there are two interrogators standing in front of Rafiq, the mentally disabled young man we took from the conventional forces weeks ago in Kirkuk. I tune in.

"We know that you are faking!" one interrogator yells.

"Quit with the fucking act!" the other chimes in.

"We're not falling for that retarded bullshit!"

"You shook your head yes when we asked if you were acting!"

I race to find Steve in the 'Gator Pit.

"Hey, why are they interrogating that mentally handicapped kid?" I ask. "Mike and I checked out the story with his brothers in Kirkuk and the Doc agreed that he's disabled."

"I know," Steve says. "Those interrogators are not on our team. They are convinced he's faking."

"He's disabled!" I say.

"I know," Steve replies. "I've had a run-in with those guys before and one of them tried to pull rank on me."

"There is no rank here," I say. "You're the senior 'gator."

"Right," Steve says, "but they don't work for me."

The interrogations of Rafiq continue unabated until a week later, when he is transferred to Abu Ghraib.

Later in the day I'm approached by Steve in the hallway.

"Did you hear what happened to Mike?" he asks.

My heart sinks.

"What? Is he okay?"

"His Stryker got hit by a roadside bomb."

I rush to a phone and dial the number to our office in Kirkuk. Mike answers.

"Yeah," he says, "we took a direct hit. It knocked us clear off the road but no one was hurt. They had to tow the Stryker back to the base."

I recall the ceremony we had two months ago for the heroes of this war. The men who gave their lives in the pursuit of terrorists like Mahmoud.

The next day the order comes down and we shave our beards.

EPILOGUE

*The answer [to the uprising] lies not in pouring more troops
into the jungle, but in the hearts and minds of the people.*
— GENERAL SIR GERALD TEMPLER,
TIGER OF MALAYA, 1952

You might have noticed that not a shot was fired by
the elite soldiers who conducted the kill-or-capture
missions while hunting Mahmoud. That is a testament
to their professionalism and competence. The insurgents
we captured didn't have time to arm themselves with a
weapon, or worse, a bomb because of the stealth and
speed of these elite soldiers. Of course, as an interrogator,
I want everyone captured alive so that I can elicit more
intelligence information that will lead to another capture.

I don't know all there is to know about interrogations.
No one does. Even since leaving Iraq and meeting other
interrogators, I've learned new techniques. Little has been
done scientifically to improve interrogation methods,
but that process is starting due to the efforts of our country's most intelligent, knowledgeable interrogator, Colonel

Steve Kleinman, an intelligence officer with over two and a half decades of experience. Colonel Kleinman and some university professors are improving our interrogation capabilities based on scientific research and American ingenuity. Since first writing about interrogations, I have met several Americans dedicated to improving the craft, and it continues to be an evolving field.

There are, however, ways in which we can improve interrogations immediately. For example, there are noncoercive law enforcement techniques that thousands of detectives and criminal investigators in the United States use every day while conducting interviews that are not being used by intelligence interrogators. The Army Field Manual was designed to interrogate rank-and-file soldiers of the Cold War, but that is not to say that it doesn't have approaches that are effective against members of al Qaeda. The techniques that we used to great success in Iraq, especially during time-sensitive interrogations at the point-of-capture, were usually ones that we had learned in the field of criminal investigations. When we mix together the approaches in the Army Field Manual with these criminal investigative techniques and tailor them to our enemy's culture, we give ourselves the best chance for success.

The other way we can rapidly improve our interrogation techniques is through cultural knowledge. Interrogators need to learn more than just facts in a classroom setting. They require exposure and we should spend the necessary resources to hire experts in culture, especially Muslims and Arabs, to instruct on these concepts. The widespread belief in misguided stereotypes about Muslims and Arabs was the single most detrimental factor to effective interrogations in Iraq. To this day, I still routinely hear politicians and pundits spreading what can only be described as ignorance and prejudices that doom our young interrogators to failure.

There is an ongoing debate about interrogation techniques in the United States and each time there is an attempted terrorist attack, some Americans renew the call for the right to torture and abuse detainees. Professional, experienced interrogators reject those calls.

The argument that the supporters of torture make is that torture and abuse are necessary to save lives. That is a lie. There is no evidence that torture and abuse are more effective or efficient than the techniques I discuss in this book. In fact, there's plenty of evidence to show that it slows the progress of the interrogation or results in bad information. Those are just the short-term problems that are created. The more significant issue is the long-term negative consequences of using torture and abuse, which are undeniable.

First, it recruits fighters for the enemy. Second, it makes future detainees less likely to cooperate because they view us as torturers. Third, it makes American soldiers captured in future conflicts vulnerable to the same techniques. Fourth, it makes opponents less willing to surrender. Finally, it lowers us to the level of our enemies.

The arguments that justify torture are unique to interrogators. When American infantrymen face resistance in battle, they aren't offered the option of breaking the law, even when it will save lives. Our best interrogators are just as capable of getting information as our most elite soldiers are at shooting targets. We don't need shortcuts.

Americans can go to sleep every night knowing that there are brave men and women out there every day convincing terrorists to cooperate. They deserve our respect and the best way to give that to them is to trust them to do their jobs.

Just as no soldier can shoot every target, no interrogator can get every detainee to talk, but that's no reason to sacrifice our principles. This conflict is as much about preserving those principles as it is about our security. And when it ends, we can proudly tell our children that we fought and won as Americans.

American interrogators are vitally important to stopping terrorist attacks, but preventive measures are not the answer to violent extremism. The end of this conflict will not come as a result of killing terrorists or denying them safe havens. They have proven that they can plan and execute missions from anywhere. We will defeat al Qaeda by denying them their lifeblood—new recruits. We should leverage our instruments of power toward achieving this strategic goal. The real battle is for the hearts and minds of al Qaeda's potential applicants.

I'm confident it is one we can win.

ACKNOWLEDGMENTS

I owe immense gratitude to my agent, Ted Weinstein, for reinventing and shaping this book. His powers of persuasion and fine intellect have convinced me that he could have a second career as an interrogator. My editor, Marc Resnick, finely tuned this small piece of war history and deserves great credit as well.

My family and friends were supportive throughout my writing. I especially thank my "second family," with whom I lived during the month in which I wrote the original manuscript, and my cousin "K." I'm indebted to my friends such as fellow Iraq veteran, and trusted reader, Val, and fellow air force veterans Roz and James. Those who have been there understand best. Thanks also to Barry Eisler, a fellow author, and David Danzig, of Human Rights First, for their support.

ACKNOWLEDGMENTS

My largest gratitude goes to my interrogations partner in Iraq, "Mike," our interpreters, Biggie and Tiny, and the soldiers of my unit. Readers will note that Mike's quick thinking was often the key to the accomplishment of our mission. One of my proudest moments of military service was awarding him the Bronze Star medal in front of his family and friends after we returned from the war.

American soldiers owe thanks to the men and women in uniform who went before us and a few men I've met since returning from the war have inspired me to continue to promote interrogators as proud professionals. Colonel Steve Kleinman, U.S. Air Force Reserve, is one of our country's smartest and most knowledgeable interrogators and displayed heroic integrity (Billy Mitchell–like) in Iraq. If there was ever a man who best understood the art and science of interrogation, it is Colonel Kleinman. Colonel Stuart Herrington is a veteran of Vietnam, Panama, and Operation Desert Storm, and is a national asset. His book, *Stalking the Vietcong,* is a must-read for interrogators. There are many other veterans that I have met, too many to mention, that also deserve thanks.

Additionally, I am deeply grateful to our World War II veterans. They set the bar high. Peter Weiss worked as a translator at the secretive Fort Hunt POW facility during World War II and reminded me that we can never become our enemies in trying to defeat them. I'm proud to follow in the footsteps of these brave Americans.

278

ACKNOWLEDGMENTS

This book would never have been possible without the support of a fellowship from the Open Society Institute. Although my work for that fellowship was separate from this book, they gave me a home from which to research and advocate for the advancement of noncoercive interrogation methods while I finished this manuscript. I could not have been more impressed with the intellect and heart of the people in the Open Society Institute. To learn more visit www.soros.org.

If you would like to learn more about interrogations, please visit www.interrogationscentral.com.

In closing, there is a way to show appreciation for all of our veterans. Please consider contributing to one of the many nonprofit organizations that takes care of our wounded war vets, such as the Yellow Ribbon Fund. Learn more at www.yellowribbonfund.com.

APPENDIX

Submitted testimony read by Senator Sheldon Whitehouse, Chair of the Senate Judiciary Committee Hearing,
on May 13, 2009: "What Went Wrong: Torture and the
Office of Legal Counsel in the Bush Administration."

Chairman Leahy and Esteemed Members of the Committee,

Thank you for the opportunity to address the Committee on the issue of interrogation. I especially thank
Senator Sheldon Whitehouse for his invitation to submit
this written testimony.

I submit this testimony as a private citizen and not as
an official representative of the United States Air Force or
as a representative of the Department of Defense. I am
currently still in the Air Force Reserves. I have served for
seventeen years in the United States Air Force and Air
Force Reserves and have completed five combat deployments to three wars. I feel that nothing less than our national soul is at stake in the debate concerning the torture
and abuse of prisoners.

In 2006, I deployed to Iraq as an interrogator at the bequest of the Army. Prior to my deployment I was a special agent for the Air Force Office of Special Investigations, both on Active Duty and in the Reserves. Before I was a special agent, I was a special operations helicopter pilot. I've served in the conflicts in Bosnia, Kosovo, Colombia, and Iraq.

As an interrogator in Iraq, I conducted more than 300 interrogations and supervised more than 1,000. I led the interrogations team that located Abu Musab al-Zarqawi, the former leader of al Qaeda in Iraq, and one of the most notorious mass murderers of our generation. At the time that we killed Zarqawi, he was the number one priority for the United States military, higher than Osama bin Laden.

I strongly oppose the use of torture or abuse as interrogation methods for both pragmatic and moral reasons. For purposes of clarity, I endorse the semantic clarification offered by Alberto Mora, former General Counsel to the Department of the Navy, who states that cruelty is a more accurate term than abuse, citing the prohibition against cruelty in the Eighth Amendment to the U.S. Constitution. For the purpose of this testimony, however, I will use the commonly used term "abuse" instead of the word "cruelty" to denote those actions that are prohibited by the U.S. Constitution, Geneva Conventions, or U.S. military regulations.

There are many pragmatic arguments against torture and abuse. The first is the lack of evidence that torture or abuse as an interrogation tactic is faster or more efficient than other methods such as relationship building or deception. In my experience, when interrogators used harsh methods that fit the definition of abuse, in every instance, that method served only to harden the resolve of the detainee and made them more resistant to interrogation. As revealed in the so-called Torture Memos, the mere fact that Khalid Sheikh Mohammad was waterboarded 183 times is ample evidence that torture made him more resistant to interrogation and that because coercion was used, he gave only the minimum amount of information necessary to stop the pain.

The second pragmatic argument against torture and abuse is the fact that al Qaeda used our policy that authorized and encouraged these illegal methods as their number one recruiting tool for foreign fighters. While I supervised interrogations in Iraq, I listened to a majority of foreign fighters state that the reason they had come to Iraq to fight was because of the torture and abuse committed at both Abu Ghraib and Guantanamo Bay. These foreign fighters made up approximately 90% of the suicide bombers in Iraq at that time, in addition to leading and participating in thousands of attacks against Coalition and Iraqi forces. It is not an exaggeration to say that hundreds, if not thousands, of American soldiers died at the hands of these foreign fighters. The policy that authorized and encouraged the torture and abuse of prisoners has cost us American lives. The torture and abuse of prisoners is counterproductive to our efforts to thwart terrorist attacks in the long term and to keep all Americans safe.

In addition, torture and abuse of prisoners causes present and future detainees to be more resistant to interrogations. When we torture or abuse detainees, it hardens their resolve and reinforces the reasons why they picked up arms against us. In addition, it makes all Americans appear as hypocrites, thereby betraying the trust that is necessary to establish prior to convincing a detainee to cooperate. Detainees are more likely to cooperate when they see us live up to our principles. Several high-ranking al Qaeda members that I interrogated in Iraq decided to cooperate with me for the very reason that I did not torture or abuse them and because I treated them and their religion and culture with respect. In fact, that was one of the main reasons I was able to convince a member of Zarqawi's inner circle to cooperate with us.

The final pragmatic argument that I offer against torture and abuse is that future adversaries will be less likely to surrender to us during combat. During the first Gulf War, thousands of Iraqi troops surrendered to American forces knowing that they would be fairly treated as prisoners of war. This same rationale was present during

World War II, where German soldiers fought and evaded in the vicinity of Berlin for the privilege of being captured by American versus Russian troops. If future adversaries are unwilling to surrender to us because of the manner in which we've treated prisoners in the current conflict, it will have a real cost in American lives.

As a military officer, it is my obligation not just to point out the broken wheel, but to fix it. So allow me to address the effective interrogation methods that led to the successes of my team in Iraq. World War II interrogators used relationship-building approaches to great success against captured Germans and Japanese, and my team imitated their methods. However, we also added new techniques to our arsenal.

I deployed to the war with four other Air Force special agents with experience as criminal investigators and we brought with us skills and training that were unique compared to our Army counterparts. Through the Air Force, we had learned to interrogate criminal suspects using relationship building and noncoercive police investigative techniques. I learned quickly in Iraq that al Qaeda has much more in common with criminal organizations than with traditional rank and file soldiers. The interrogation methods in the Army Field Manual 2-22.3 are valid approaches and sometimes applicable for interrogating members of al Qaeda, but even more effective are the techniques that I learned as a criminal investigator. I used these techniques, permitted by the Army Manual under the terms "... psychological ploys, verbal trickery, or other nonviolent or non-coercive subterfuge ..." to great success and I taught these techniques to other members of my interrogation team. Just one example of a commonly used criminal investigative technique that has been adopted into the Army Field Manual is the Good Cop/Bad Cop approach, but there are numerous others that are absent from both the manual and the Army's interrogator training. The U.S. law enforcement community has much to add to the improvement of our interrogation methods and the United States Army would do well to consult with experienced criminal investigators from our police departments and federal law enforcement agencies.

I also want to address the so-called "ticking time bomb" scenario that is so often used as an excuse for torture and abuse. My team lived through this scenario every day in Iraq. The men that we captured and interrogated were behind Zarqawi's suicide bombing campaign. Most of our prisoners had knowledge of future suicide bombing operations that could have been prevented with the quick extraction of accurate intelligence information. Even if we assume that torture or abuse are more effective or efficient than other methods of interrogation, which in my experience they are not, my team knew that we could not save lives today at the expense of losing lives tomorrow. We knew that we would be recruiting future fighters for al Qaeda's ranks, some of whom would surely kill Americans and other innocent civilians and, most likely, our brothers and sisters in arms.

What works best in the ticking time bomb scenario is relationship building, which is not a time-consuming effort when conducted by a properly trained interrogator, and noncoercive deception. By reciting a line from the Quran at the beginning of an interrogation, I often built rapport in a matter of minutes. Contrary to popular belief, building a relationship with a prisoner is not necessarily a time consuming exercise.

I also conducted point-of-capture interrogations in Iraqi homes, streets, and cars, and I discovered that in these time-constrained environments where an interrogator has ten or fifteen minutes to assess a detainee and obtain accurate intelligence information, relationship building and deception were again the most effective interrogation tools. It is about being smarter, not harsher.

I have addressed the pragmatic arguments against torture and abuse and discussed effective noncoercive interrogation methods, but let me address the more important issue in this debate—the moral argument against torture and abuse. When I took the oath of office as a military officer, I swore to uphold and defend the Constitution of the United States of America, which specifically prohibits cruelty towards any person in the Eighth Amendment. In addition, torture and abuse are inconsistent with the basic principles of freedom, liberty, and justice, upon which our country was founded. George Washington, during the Revolutionary War, specifically prohibited his troops from torturing prisoners. Abraham Lincoln prohibited Union troops from torturing Confederate prisoners. We have a long history of abiding by American principles while conducting war.

Some have argued that the arguments against torture and abuse are clear on a "sunny day" in 2009 versus after the dark cloud of 9/11. There is no mention of sunny days versus dark days in the military officer's oath of office. As leaders, military officers bear the responsibility to keep their emotions in check and to fulfill their duties consistent with American principles. I can offer no better words than those of General George C. Marshall, the orchestrator of the Allied victory in Europe during World War II, who stated, "Once an army is involved in war, there is a beast in every fighting man which begins tugging at its chains . . . a good officer must learn early on how to keep the beast under control, both in his men and in himself."

As a proud American, I know that we have the intellectual ability to defeat our enemies in the battle of wits in the interrogation room. We will not convince every detainee to cooperate, but we can lose battles and still win the war. No profession can boast of perfect performance in combat—infantry soldiers don't shoot every target. On the road to Zarqawi, my interrogation team encountered several high-ranking members of al Qaeda who did not cooperate, but we used those interrogations as opportunities to improve our skills. In fact, it was in one such case that I developed a noncoercive technique that I later used on the detainee who led us to Zarqawi.

We are smart enough to effectively interrogate our adversaries and we should not doubt our ability to convince detainees to cooperate. American culture gives us unique advantages that we can leverage during interrogations—tolerance, cultural understanding, intellect, and ingenuity. In closing, the same qualities that make us great Americans will make us great interrogators.

I want to thank the Committee again for this opportunity to submit testimony based on my experiences.

Respectfully,
Matthew Alexander

THE INTERROGATOR'S CODE

1. The first and most important victory is to get inside the mind and heart of the prisoner.

2. Never forget that the prisoner walks into the room with as many information requirements as the interrogator. What ensues is a negotiation.

3. An innocent man may have no information, but he can tell you what questions to ask. He'll never do that unless you treat him with respect.

4. Better to make the prisoner forget you are enemies than to remind him.

5. If you've exhausted your approach and it isn't working, try the exact opposite—even if it doesn't make sense.

6. Never rule out love of family.

7. Culture is compulsory.

8. Have sympathetic common sense.

9. The higher the rank, the more they talk.

10. During war, individuals on either side are drawn to talk to one another like magnets.

11. A good interrogator is one-third actor, one-third psychiatrist, and one-third salesman.

12. Always afford a prisoner the opportunity to tell *his* side of the story.

13. Maslow was 50 percent correct.

14. Bait your hook to suit your fish.

15. Anyone who says, "The prisoner is definitely lying," is definitely guessing.

16. If he is talking, you are winning.